THE PARAMETERS OF POSITIVITY

All Dreams can come True as long as you don't Sleep on Them

L. STANLEY BASCOMB

Printed in the United States of America

ISBN 979-8-89114-215-2 (sc)
ISBN 979-8-89114-216-9 (e)

Library of Congress Preassigned Control Number: 2025914634

2025.08.18

MainSpring Books
5901 W. Century Blvd
Suite 750
Los Angeles, CA, US, 90045

www.mainspringbooks.com

DEDICATION

Along with my poems and thoughts and actions, I hope that there are positive thoughts,

That I can or have already brought to my Family and Friends and maybe to someone in this world…..

I dedicate this book to my son,
Javontae Devon Bascomb

You have brought to me nothing but joy, humbleness and an appreciation for the kind of person that you have become, you have taken your own road without disrespecting others, I have watched you grow into a young dedicated black man, you didn't have to play sports or act gangster to prove how much heart you had, you have just been you, SPECIAL!

You have been my HERO!

CONTENTS

It's Time 1

Starting All Over Again 4

Giving Back to Black 7

I Don't Understand 9

SPIRITUAL POEMS

A Poem 4 Me 14

Bridge Over Troubled Waters 16

Dream...19

Heaven & Earth 20

If You Ever Lost A Friend Like Mine............... 21

I'm in Me 23

It's Time 25

Love Can Be Lonely 2................................... 27

Now It's Your Time.. 28

Respect Appreciate Understand 30

Storm and Breeze 32

The Light... 34

True To Yourself.. 36

When I Go Away.. 38

FAMILY POEMS

A Father Of One Of Three Children 42

Feel Me Everyday Family................................. 47

Forever Ours 49

I Am You.. 50

Javontae Bascomb.................................... 52

Last Night.. 53

Love.. 56

Mother Extraordinaire 58

My Family You Are 61

My Love.. 63

On To The Next One 64

Our Brother, Our Wonder, ... 66

US... 68

What I Am... 70

When I'm Not Here! Can I! 72

When Will We Love Us 75

You Don't Owe Me.................................... 78

Your Silent Whisper of Love........................... 80

THOUGHTFUL POEMS

Appreciation... 84

Blacker Before 87

Common Ground...91

Nubian Queen..94

Pray for Our Children 97

Thank You 101

The World Today 102

LOVE POEMS

Am I A Fool.. 104

Chance Love 106

Did You Know?... 108

Do You Have A Man...................................... 110

Do You Really Have The Time 112

Endings 114

Eyes 116

Free Flowin Poem 4 U 118

Hurt Unhurt 120

Hurts So Good 122

I Wrote This Poem 4 U 124

If I..128

If You Ever Wondered.................................. 130

If 133

It's You 135

Lovin Time 137

My Soul Is In The Creator's Hands

My Heart Is In Yours...................................... 140

New Beginning 144

Our Love 146

Please Don't Dislike Me, I Am Just A Man...................147

Reaching Up, Reaching Out....................................... 150

Reality Of Love...152

Special 155

The Beauty Of U..156

Touch... 158

Why? 159

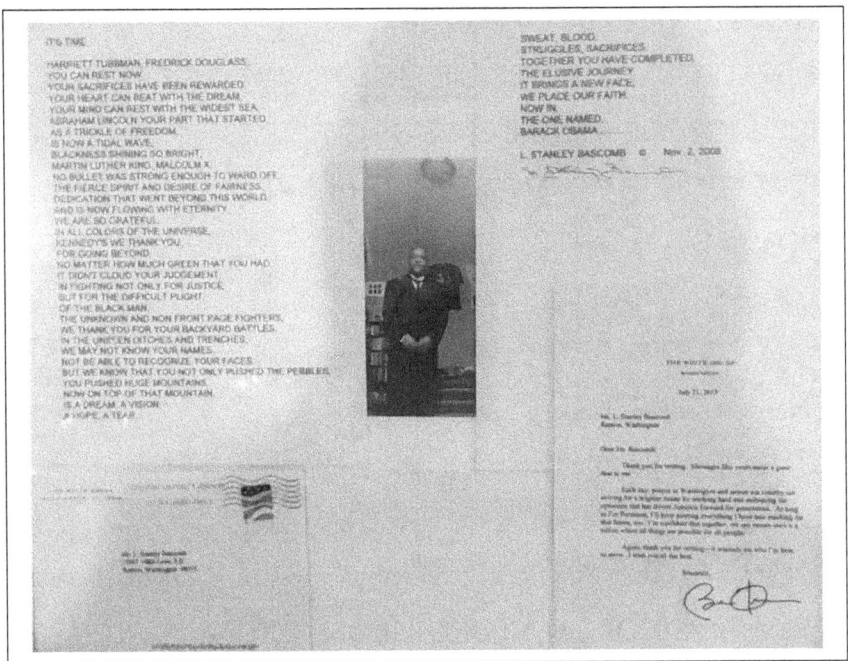

IT'S TIME

HARRIETT TUBBMAN, FREDRICK DOUGLASS,

YOU CAN REST NOW,

YOUR SACRIFICES HAVE BEEN REWARDED,

YOUR HEART CAN BEAT WITH THE DREAM,

YOUR MIND CAN REST WITH THE WIDEST SEA,

ABRAHAM LINCOLN YOUR PART THAT STARTED,

AS A TRICKLE OF FREEDOM,

IS NOW A TIDAL WAVE,

BLACKNESS SHINING SO BRIGHT,

MARTIN LUTHER KING, MALCOLM X,

NO BULLET WAS STRONG ENOUGH TO WARD OFF,

THE FIERCE SPIRIT AND DESIRE OF FAIRNESS,

DEDICATION THAT WENT BEYOND THIS WORLD,

AND IS NOW FLOWING WITH ETERNITY,

WE ARE SO GRATEFUL,

IN ALL COLORS OF THE UNIVERSE,

KENNEDY'S WE THANK YOU,

FOR GOING BEYOND,

NO MATTER HOW MUCH GREEN THAT YOU HAD,

IT DIDN'T CLOUD YOUR JUDGEMENT,

IN FIGHTING NOT ONLY FOR JUSTICE,

BUT FOR THE DIFFICULT PLIGHT,

OF THE BLACK MAN,

THE UNKNOWN AND NON FRONT PAGE FIGHTERS,

WE THANK YOU FOR YOUR BACKYARD BATTLES,

IN THE UNSEEN DITCHES AND TRENCHES,

WE MAY NOT KNOW YOUR NAMES,

NOT BE ABLE TO RECOGNIZE YOUR FACES,

BUT WE KNOW THAT YOU NOT ONLY PUSHED THE PEBBLES,

YOU PUSHED HUGE MOUNTAINS,

NOW ON TOP OF THAT MOUNTAIN,

IS A DREAM, A VISION,

A HOPE, A TEAR,

SWEAT, BLOOD,

STRUGGLES, SACRIFICES,

TOGETHER YOU HAVE COMPLETED,

THE ELUSIVE JOURNEY,

IT BRINGS A NEW FACE,

WE PLACE OUR FAITH,

NOW IN,

THE ONE NAMED,

BARACK OBAMA..........

L. STANLEY BASCOMB © Nov. 2, 2008

STARTING
ALL OVER AGAIN

We as parents must understand,

We are the architects of our children's,

Many collective steps of achievements or failures,

Their actual first physical steps were a joy to us all,

Then we tended to take them for granted,

We forgot that they needed us every step of the way,

As parent we have been there before,

But now! We are starting all over again through them,

This is our chance to make the rough roads,

We faced smooth for them,

A chance to help wipe out the ignorance and prejudice,

To let them know, to be different is a blessing,

Also, that because you might look different outside,

It is that's inside of you that counts,

As the skies are made up of different shapes,

Without clouds stars sun and moon,

There wouldn't be any sky to appreciate,

These children are our future,

Right now, they rely on us for guidance,

The guidance we give them today,

We will rely on them for our future tomorrow,

We must make them competitive,

But teach them fairness,

We want them on top,

But be compassionate for those who aren't,

We want them to be outgoing,

But teach them safety,

We want them to be independent,

But they must know,

Can't take freedom for granted,

Be vigilant, aware, observant,

That we as parents,

We as family,

Are there for them,

This is our chance as parents,

To right the wrongs,

Of the past,

Give them a chance to make the future,

Positive, hopeful,

Make the sacrifices, not a sacrifice,

These children are our chance of wiping,

The chalkboard clean,

Give hope to the world,

That is real for us,

Along with others,

Children today have more information available than,

We had at their age,

Let's give them a chance to use it wisely,

We've cured almost every disease created,

Except for the one some humans made themselves,

Ignorance, selfishness, and prejudice,

Maybe if we pass along enough votes,

The final one will say,

Love, Peace and Togetherness,

Our children have a chance,

To make a better world for themselves and us,

But they need us to help them..........

L. Stanley Bascomb © 2007

GIVING BACK TO BLACK

In my efforts to bring a positive spirit to our next black generation, in using football as my tool, every player isn't going to be a professional football player, they may not even be a high school player, but they must be taught and understand, self, respect and the respect of others, to have an appreciation of difference, setting goals to achieve success, learn to work with each other as young black men, if I can take 11 young black men to learn to get a football across a goal line and defend a goal line.

We as a people should be able to take those same young black men be able together learn the field of life.

I also have cautioned my coaches to be careful how they treat each individual young man, we don't know his life, his history, his wants or needs,

They are in our care for only 2 hours a day, that 2 hours might be the only positive 2 hours in that child's daily life,

If we can give them enough positiveness in those 2 hours, that will give them the belief that there is hope for another 22 hours of hope in their future.

For all those recognized as great people in this world, sometimes there is a beginning where you have no recognition, let's start giving our young youth a face they can start recognizing today for their future tomorrow..........
LSB © March 17, 2019

I write this because this is my life's experience growing up in my community, this can be relevant in any community in order to provide a positive next generation for the future, it might start in your hood, but at some point, it will become a part of the world..........

I DON'T UNDERSTAND

HELLO MY YOUNG BLACK BROTHERS,

I'M AN OLDER BLACK MAN,

BORN POOR LIKE YOU,

BUT I DON'T UNDERSTAND YOUR PLAN,

PLEASE YOUNG BROTHERS,

PUT DOWN THE GUNS,

BEFORE THE NIGHT,

DEAD IS ANOTHER BLACK MOTHER'S SON,

YES!

I KNOW YO WANT TO IMPRESS OTHERS,

BUT IF WE KILL US,

THERE'S NO ONE ELSE TO CALL BROTHER,

WHEN YOU SHOOT SOMEONE,

THAT IS THE END,

TOMORROW HE HAS NO CHANCE,

TO BE YOUR FRIEND,

THE NEXT YOUNG BROTHER,

HAS NO MORE THAN YOU,

WHY TAKE HIS LIFE,

TOGETHER,

BOTH YOUR DREAMS,

COULD HAVE COME TRUE,

I HAVE LIVED WITH YOUR HURT,

I UNDERSTAND YOUR FRUSTRATION,

BUT IF WE KEEP GOING LIKE THIS,

THERE MIGHT NOT BE,

ANOTHER BLACK GENERATION,

YOU THINK DRUGS AND GUNS ARE MIGHT,

OLDER BLACKS GAVE LIVES AND SOULS,

FOR YOU TO HAVE YOUR RIGHTS,

MALCOLM X, MANDELA, MUHAMMAD ALI, DR. KING,

BROTHERS WHO HAVE FOUGHT FOR YOU,

NOW LET'S DO THE RIGHT THING,

NO!

THEY DON'T HAVE ALL THE ANSWERS,

IT'S TIME FOR YOU TO PAY YOUR DUES,

TOGETHER WE CAN FIND ALL THE ANSWERS,

I CAN ONLY FIND A FEW,

PLEASE PUT DOWN THE GUNS G.,

MAKE ANOTHER PLAN,

LET THE CHILDREN FEEL FREE,

FUNERALS, GUNS, COLORS, CRACK,

PLEASE YOUNG BROTHERS,

YOU NEED TO COME BACK,

TO BEING YOUNG GIFTED AND BLACK,

YOUNG, YOUNG, BROTHERS,

I DON'T UNDERSTAND YOUR PLAN,

PLEASE LET THAT YOUNG BLACK,

TURN INTO,

A BEAUTIFUL BLACK MAN..........

L. STANLEY BASCOMB © 1995

SPIRITUAL POEMS

A POEM 4 ME

I LIVED IN DARKNESS AS A CHILD,

MY SOUL WAS SO VERY MEEK,

TIMID AND MILD,

I HAD TO FORSAKE THAT SOUL,

TO BECOME A MAN,

LIFE WAS A BLUR,

I DIDN'T ALWAYS HAVE,

THE BEST OR BRIGHTEST PLANS,

AT TIMES I WAS TOLD,

I WAS GOING TO HELL,

BECAUSE MY SPIRIT,

QUESTIONED,

THE BIBLES TALE,

IN MY LIFE'S BEGINNING,

SO MANY BURDENS,

IN A VERY YOUNG BOY,

THAT HAD NO DEFINITION,

OR CONCEPT OF BEING,

A MAN,

IN MY SOUL,

I DREAMED OF BEING LOVED,

HELD BY PRECIOUS HANDS,

LOVE HAS BEEN MY KRYPTONITE,

WISHING AND LONGING FOR IT,

VERTUALLY EVERY,
DAY AND NIGHT,
PART OF MY LIFE,
CONFUSED BY LOVE AND SEX,
JUST GOING WITH,
WHAT FEMALE WAS NEXT,
EYESIGHT CAN BLIND YOU,
A TOUCH CAN DECIEVE YOU,
MY SPIRIT,
IS NATURE THAT GUIDES ME,
MY SOUL,
IS INFORMATION FROM MY LIFE,
MY COMPASS, MY DESTINATION,
ONLY I CAN,
FEEL AND EXAMINE,
MY EXPERIENCES,
MY BELIEF IN ME,
CAN PROTECT ME FOREVER,
FROM THE HURT,
FROM HUMAN TEACHING,
LIFE IS SIMPLY LIFE,
LIVE YOURS,
I AM GOOD,
WITH MINE..........

L. STANLEY BASCOMB
September 16, 2019 ©

BRIDGE OVER
TROUBLED WATERS

YOU ARE THE ARCHITECT,

STRENGTH OF THE BEAMS,

HOW LONG HAVE YOU BEEN THERE,

I KNOW!

FOREVER IT SEEMS,

YOU ARE THE BOLTS,

THAT HOLD IT STRONG,

WHY? WHY?

IS IT YOU,

THAT HEARS THAT LAST SONG,

YOU BRIDGE THE GAP,

BETWEEN HERE AND THERE,

FAMILY LOOKS TO YOU FOR STRENGTH,

SOMETIMES YOU WONDER,

IS IT FAIR,

YOU ARE THE SPAN,

THAT GIVE MANY A HUG,

YOU SIT HIGH ABOVE,

MORE STRENGTH THAN ANY TUG,

MANY STAND ON YOU,

LOOKING ACROSS THE SEA,

SOMETIMES TAKING YOU FOR GRANTED,

YOUR STRONG EXTERIOR,

DISGUISES YOUR FRAGILE BEAUTY,

YOU PAINT YOURSELF,

WITH STRENGTH EACH DAY,

WHEN YOU FEEL WEATHER BEATEN,

OUT FROM THE CLOUDS,

COMES A SUN RAY,

YOU'VE BEEN MORE THAN A FRIEND,

I PRAY AND HOPE,

YOU WILL BE HERE,

EVEN PAST MY END,

YOU ARE A LIVING MARTYR,

YOU HAVE BEEN THE BRIDGE,

OVER A SMOOTH AND ROUGH WATERS..........

DEDICATED TO AUNT MARGUARITE VADEN

L. STANLEY BASCOMB © 1995

DREAM

A STAR IN THE SKY,

SHINES SO BRIGHT,

IT SITS IN HEAVEN,

GLOWING THROUGH THE NIGHT,

FAR AWAY AS IT MAY SEEM,

YOU WISH UPON IT,

TO FULFILL YOUR DREAMS,

THOUGH MY DREAM IS NOT HERE,

I STILL LOOK UPON THAT STAR,

SO, VERY, VERY, NEAR..........

L. STANLEY BASCOMB © 1992

HEAVEN & EARTH

I HAVE LAUGHED AND SMILED,

WITH MANY,

MANY HAVE LAUGHED AND SMILED,

WITH ME,

THAT HAS BEEN MY HEAVEN,

ON EARTH...........

L. STANLEY BASCOMB © July 5, 2016

IF YOU EVER LOST A FRIEND LIKE MINE

IF YOU EVER LOST A FRIEND LIKE MINE,

A FRIEND THAT EXTENDS PAST TIME,

THAT YOU CAN TALK WITH,

THAT YOU CAN WALK WITH,

THAT YOU CAN SHARE YOUR MINDS,

AND NO ONE HAS TO SPEAK ABOUT THE HEART,

IT'S SOMETHING THAT YOU JUST SHARE,

AS FRIENDS,

FROM THE VERY START,

YOU DON'T EVEN THINK ABOUT,

WHEN YOU FIRST BECAME FRIENDS,

IT WAS JUST A NATURAL,

LIKE WHEN BABIES ARE BORN TWINS,

YOU ARE MORE THAT JUST MY FRIEND,

YOU ARE MY BROTHER,

MY SPIRIT, MY SOUL,

WE RAN, THE STREETS,

DID THINGS LIKE NO OTHERS COULD DO,

WE WERE SHARPER THAN TACKS,

KNOWING THAT FOREVER,

NO MATTER THE SITUATION,

WE HAD EACH OTHERS BACKS,

SOME STILL DON'T UNDERSTAND,

THIS MAN IS STILL MY FRIEND,

EVEN PAST EARTHS END,

I AM STILL RAINING TEARS OF SORROW,

I WILL NEVER SEE,

MY FRIEND TOMORROW,

YOU GOT THERE FIRST,

I KNOW THAT YOU WILL,

HOLD A PLACE FOR ME,

WE'LL TAKE IT FROM THE STREETS,

PAST SATURN, VENUS, MARS,

PAST ETERITY..........

L. STANLEY BASCOMB © JUNE 10, 2014

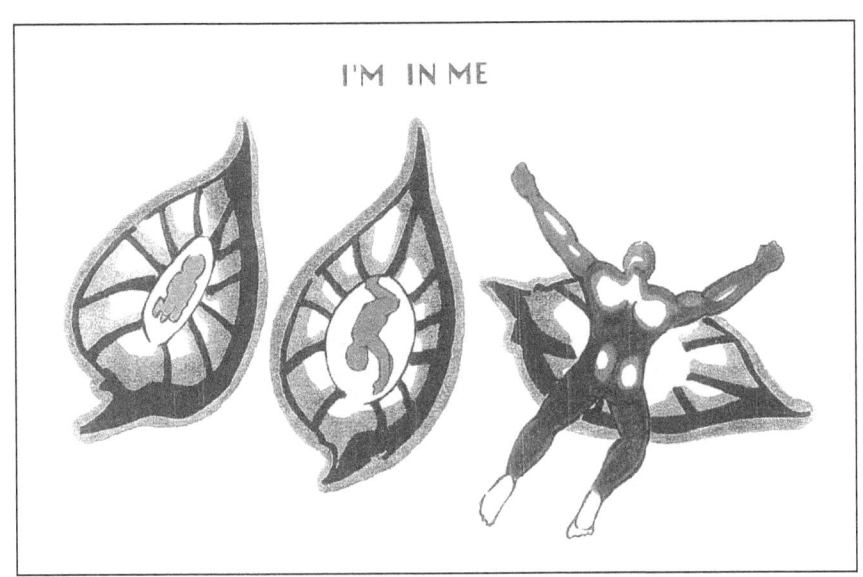

I'M IN ME

HERE I STAND ON A LEAF,

WHICH WAY DO I GO,

NOT KNOWING WHAT'S BENEATH,

I HAVE TO EAT,

BUT I CAN'T EAT THIS LEAF,

NOT KNOWING WHAT'S BENEATH,

I HAVE ALL THESE LEGS TO CARRY,

AT TIMES I WISH THEY WEREN'T,

CAUSE AT TIMES I'M SO WEARY,

I LOOK BELOW, EVERYTHING IS AMUCK,

I WAS ONCE DOWN THERE,

ALMOST GOT ATE UP,

UP ABOVE IT SEEMS SO FREE,

THEY HAVE ALL THE LUCK,

HOW CAN I GET THERE,

HOW CAN I BE ME AND ALSO FREE,

I TOOK A LONG SLEEP,

DREAMED THAT I BELIEVED I ME,

AS I AWOKE,

I FELT SUCH A CHANGE,

I WAS STILL ON THAT LEAF,

I LOOKED,

I HAD A PAIR OF WINGS,

SO BEAUTIFUL, SO SERENE,

DIDN'T FEEL WARY,

NOT SO MANY LEGS TO CARRY,

HERE I AM FREE, FREE, FREE,

WAS IT THE DREAM,

OR,

WAS IT ALWAYS THERE TO BE,

OR,

WAS IT IFINALLY BELIEVED IN ME..........

L. STANLEY BASCOMB © 1992

IT'S TIME

HARRIETT TUBBMAN, FREDRICK DOUGLASS,

YOU CAN REST NOW,

YOUR SACRIFICES HAVE BEEN REWARDED,

YOUR HEART CAN BEAT WITH THE DREAM,

YOUR MIND CAN REST WITH THE WIDEST SEA,

ABRAHAM LINCOLN YOUR PART THAT STARTED,

AS A TRICKLE OF FREEDOM,

IS NOW A TIDAL WAVE,

BLACKNESS SHINING SO BRIGHT,

MARTIN LUTHER KING, MALCOLM X,

NO BULLET WAS STRONG ENOUGH TO WARD OFF,

THE FIERCE SPIRIT AND DESIRE OF FAIRNESS,

DEDICATION THAT WENT BEYOND THIS WORLD,

AND IS NOW FLOWING WITH ETERNITY,

WE ARE SO GRATEFUL,

IN ALL COLORS OF THE UNIVERSE,

KENNEDY'S WE THANK YOU,

FOR GOING BEYOND,

NO MATTER HOW MUCH GREEN THAT YOU HAD,

IT DIDN'T CLOUD YOUR JUDGEMENT,

IN FIGHTING NOT ONLY FOR JUSTICE,

BUT FOR THE DIFFICULT PLIGHT,

OF THE BLACK MAN,

THE UNKNOWN AND NON FRONT PAGE FIGHTERS,

WE THANK YOU FOR YOUR BACKYARD BATTLES,

IN THE UNSEEN DITCHES AND TRENCHES,

WE MAY NOT KNOW YOUR NAMES,

NOT BE ABLE TO RECOGNIZE YOUR FACES,

BUT WE KNOW THAT YOU NOT ONLY PUSHED THE PEBBLES,

YOU PUSHED HUGE MOUNTAINS,

NOW ON TOP OF THAT MOUNTAIN,

IS A DREAM, A VISION,

A HOPE, A TEAR,

SWEAT, BLOOD,

STRUGGLES, SACRIFICES,

TOGETHER YOU HAVE COMPLETED,

THE ELUSIVE JOURNEY,

IT BRINGS A NEW FACE,

WE PLACE OUR FAITH,

NOW IN,

THE ONE NAMED,

BARACK OBAMA..........

L. STANLEY BASCOMB © Nov. 2, 2008

LOVE CAN BE LONELY 2

I entered this world, not knowing a word,

The ones I brought here were just jibber,

I used my emotions, before I used my mind,

I now am a part of mankind,

There were expectations I didn't know about,

I learned to be me, in me I was the best,

But I couldn't impress mankind, I just knew me,

I knew I wasn't a butterfly or a bee,

I jut tried to spread my wings and be me,

But I soon found out even,

Love can be lonely 2

I am sure my smile, at times looked upside down,

I didn't get in the mirror, that day,

Forgive me, but you know what,

I still knew how to pray,

I have no regrets,

Love can be lonely 2

I leave you my spirit, leave you my heart,

If that brings you laughter,

Brings you a smile,

I have done my part,

For the time I was here..........

Cynthia Bascomb Jones

L. Stanley Bascomb 7/27/2021 ©

NOW IT'S YOUR TIME

YOU DON'T HAVE TO BE THAT BRIDGE OVER TROUBLED WATERS ANYMORE,

YOU DON'T HAVE TO BE THE ROCK THAT IS THE STRENGTH OF EVERYONE,

NOW IT'S YOUR TIME,

THE SKIES AND THE STARS ARE LOOKING AT YOU,

YOUR SPIRIT AND LOVE,

PURE AS THE OCEANS,

BRIGHT AS THE MORNING DEW,

WE ARE SO MUCH GOING TO MISS YOU,

YOU ALWAYS LOOKED AT THE POSITIVE,

YOU HAVE ALWAYS KEPT YOUR FAITH,

NOW IT'S YOUR TIME,

WE CAN STILL SMELL YOUR COOKING

HEAR THE SWEETNESS OF YOUR VOICE4,

SEE THE SMILE THAT BLESSED YOUR FACE,

IN LIFE YOU WERE ALWAYS UP THERE,

AS FIRST CHOICE,

YOU WERE THE MOM OF MOMS,

EVEN TO THOSE,

WHO WERE NOT BORN OF YOUR FLESH,

BUT HAD THE SPIRIT OF YOU,

YOU SHARED WITH THE COLORS,

OF EVERY HUE,

NOW IT'S YOUR TIME,

HIGH UP IN THE SKIES,

YOU HAVE THE HIGHEST VIEW,

I SAW YOU PEEK AT US,

FELT THE SOFTNESS OF YOUR HANDS,

SOUL & SPIRIT RINGING ONE MORE TIME,

NOW IT'S YOUR TIME,

NOW IT'S YOUR TIME,

DEDICATED TO AUNT MARGUARITE VADEN

L. STANLEY BASCOMB

JAN. 4, 2019 ©

RESPECT APPRECIATE UNDERSTAND

MOUNTAINS, MOLEHILLS,

VALLEYS, DITCHES,

THEY WILL STILL BE HERE,

AFTER ALL YOUR RICHES,

OCEANS, PONDS,

RIVERS, SEAS,

HEAVEN REQUIRES,

JUST A SPIRITUAL FEE,

GREET THE MORNING,

REACH YOUR HEAD TO THE SKIES,

RETURN TO YOUR SPIRIT,

NO MORE MYTHS, NO MORE LIES,

WE MUST UNDERSTAND,

WHERE WE STAND

THE CREATOR MADE US,

MAN DID NOT MAKE MAN,

DON'T LET THE MATERIAL,

STAND IN YOUR WAY,

YOU CAN GREET HEAVEN,

OR, HAVE HELL TO PAY,

RESPECT THE FLOWERS,

BIRDS AND BEES,

REMEMBER THE CREATOR,

MADE THEM AND ME,

I'M NOT HERE TO BE,

ANYONE'S BERATER,

BUT, WHY DO WE GIVE,

SO MUCH POWER TO,

A GREEN PIECE OF PAPER,

FROM A BLADE OF GRASS,

TO THE TALLEST TREE,

DOESN'T MATTER THE HEIGHT,

IT'S HOW WE LOOK,

WHAT WE REALLY WANT TO SEE,

LOOK INSIDE YOURSELF,

TO SEE WHAT WE HAVE LOST,

CAUSE WHAT YOU DON'T UNDERSTAND,

COULD BE YOUR SOULS ULTIMATE COST,

WE CREATE NOTHING,

WE BORROW FROM WHAT'S HERE,

APPRECIATE THE SENDER,

LOVE HAS NO FEAR,

GIVE A SMILE, LEND A HAND TO THEE,

RESPECT, APPRECIATE, UNDERSTAND,

ONLY ONE GREATOR MADE EVERYTHING AND MAN..........

L. STANLEY BASCOMB © 2010

STORM AND BREEZE

FLOAT WITH THE SEA,

BEND WITH THE WIND,

LOOK OVER THE MOUNTAIN,

ONE'S SOUL IS FREE,

SATURN, JUPITER, NEPTUNE,

GALAXIES SO FAR,

SHE NOT GONE,

SHE IS AMONG THE STARS,

THE CLOUDS ARE YOUR CUSHION,

THE RAIN YOUR TEARS,

THE STORM IS YOUR HURT,

WALK WITH THE BREEZE,

LOVE OF TWO,

SHE WILL EAZE YOUR FEARS,

TO SEE IS A MIRAGE,

TO TOUCH CAN DECEIVE,

TO SHARE HER LOVE,

WILL LAST PAST ETERNITY,

SHE WILL SMILE WITH LIGHTING,

SEE WITH THE SUN,

TALK WITH THUNDER,

DANCE WITH A QUAKE,

SING WITH THE BIRDS AND BEES,

HOLD YOU FOREVER,

FROM ALL STORMS,

WITH A BREEZE..........

L. STANLEY BASCOMB © 1995

THE LIGHT

THE LIGHT

YOU'VE FOLLOWED THE LIGHT THROUGH YOUR LIFE,

THE CREATOR IS BRINGING YOU HOME TO NO MORE STRIFE,

HEAR THE BELLS AS THEY TOLL,

REMEMBER NOTHING IS MORE PRECIOUS THAN YOUR SOUL,

THE BREEZE IS YOUR COMFORT FOREVER MY DEAR,

WATCHING YOU IN SPIRIT SO STRONG,

I NOW HAVE NO FEAR,

I PRAY WE SEE EACH OTHER IN SOME TIME OR SPACE,

YOUR SPOT IN MY HEART,

NO ONE WILL FILL ITS PLACE,

I HAVE NO DOUBTS WHEN YOU'RE UP ABOVE,

THERE WILL BE THE BIRTH OF A VERY SPECIAL DOVE,

THESE WORDS THAT I WRITE COMES FOM THE ALMIGHTY,

CAUSE I PRAYED AND TALKED ABOUT YOU NIGHTLY,

I ASK FOR YOUR FORGIVENESS FOR NOT COMING BEFORE,

I HAD TO FIND STRENGTH IN MYSELF,

BEFORE I CAME TO YOUR DOOR,

A PART OF ME WILL ALWAYS BE WITH YOU,

BECAUSE I PRAY ALSO, TO END UP THERE TOO,

YOU MAY FEEL WEAK NOW, BUT DON'T DESPAIR,

YOU WILL HAVE MORE STRENGTH THAN ANYONE,

WHEN YOU CLIMB UP THOSE STAIRS,

YOU WEREN'T RICH BY STANDARDS OF MONEY,

BUT YES,

YOU WERE THERE FOR OTHERS,

WHEN THINGS GOT FUNNY,

EVEN AT THIS TIME I ENVY YOU,

CAUSE YOU HAVE HELD FAITHFUL WORDS SO TRUE,

YOU WALK HAND IN HAND WITH,

THE CREATOR ON YOUR RIGHT,

AS I LOOK IN YOUR FACE,

I TOO CAN SEE THE LIGHT..........

DEDICATED TO COUSIN GLORIA JOHNSON

L. STANLEY BASCOMB © 1992

TRUE TO YOURSELF

IN ALL THE YEARS WE HAVE BEEN FAMILY,

WHICH HAS BEEN MANY, MANY, MANY,

IN A FEW MOMENTS,

I LEARNED MORE ABOUT YOUR STRENTH,

YOUR COURAGE,

YOUR DETERMINATION,

YOUR RESILENCE,

YOUR SPIRIT, YOUR SOUL,

FOR YEARS,

YOU CARRIED YOUR BURDEN,

SILENTLY,

MASKED YOUR PHYSICAL PAIN,

IN ORDER,

FOR YOUR FAMILY TO REMAIN,

THE SAME,

YOU NEVER CHANGED YOUR HEART,

YOUR PRESENCE WAS FELT BY MANY,

NOT JUST A FEW,

WE NEVER KNEW,

YOU WERE SUFFERING INSIDE,

YOU ONLY ALLOWED,

US TO SEE YOU,

THROUGH YOUR WONDERFUL SMILE,

YOU GAVE, PICNICS,

YOU ALLOWED US TO PARTY,

YOU DANCED WITH US,

IN THE MIST,

OF WHAT YOU WERE GOING THROUGH,

YOU REMAINED,

MORE POWERFUL,

THAN MUHAMMAD ALI'S FIST,

RIGHT NOW,

YOU ARE MY HERO,

THE LAST DAY,

THAT I SAW YOU,

I BREATHED YOUR AIR,

I KEPT A FEW BREATHS FOR ME,

I TOUCHED AND CARESSED,

YOUR HANDS AND FACE,

I WANTED TO MAKE SURE,

YOU STAYED A PART OF ME,

PAST MY END,

THAT WILL REMAIN THE SAME

THROUGH WHAT WE CALL ETERNITY,

YOU HAVE BEEN TRUE TO YOURSELF..........

DEDICATED TO HELEN HARPER

LOVE U

COUSIN STANLEY BASCOMB

WHEN I GO AWAY

When I go away,

Will you keep,

A part of me here,

Allow me,

A space in,

Your heart,

Let me flow,

Like a whisper in your ear,

When I go away,

Will you allow me,

To be a smile,

On your face,

A reflection,

In your eyes,

A spirit that was,

Decent,

Knowing not always right,

Will you allow me,

To reminisce in,

Your mind,

Good that we shared,

No matter what,

We went through,

In the end,

We both cared,

When I go away

I want you to know,

That you brought,

Me joy,

You were all,

That I had,

As I write this poem,

It has made me cry,

I sit in silence,

Wishing that I,

Was by your side,

When I go away,

I know that,

You don't really know me,

I may not know,

All of you,

But,

The love that I,

Have inside,

Is only meant,

For my family,

Which means,

You,

It will reflect,

With the planets above,

It will flow with the sea's,

Sit on top of,

Every mountain,

Ride the winds,

Float with the breeze,

In the Artic,

It will never freeze,

When I go away,

I don't know,

Where the journey,

Will take me,

I just know,

Where it began,

From me to you,

That my love,

Will never end..........

DEDICATED TO MY SON JAVONTAE

L. STANLEY BASCOMB © May 4, 2016

FAMILY POEMS

A FATHER OF ONE OF THREE CHILDREN

MY OFF SPRINGS ARE 3

1 DAUGHTER, 2 SONS,

I WATCHED 2 BE BORN,

1 BORN BEFORE I KNEW,

I LOVE THEM ALL,

ALL SO FRESH AND BRAND NEW,

THEY CAME HERE WITH INNOCENCE,

FUTURES SO BRIGHT,

I DID WHAT I COULD,

FROM DAY TO NIGHT,

YOU ARE MY FLESH,

YOU ARE MY BLOOD,

YOU ARE MY DREAMS,

YOU ARE MY HOPES,

I CHERISH YOU FROM,

SEA TO SEA,

MOUNTAIN TO MOUNTAIN,

WITH EVERY BREATH YOU TAKE,

I WISH YOU BREATH,

THAT TAKES YOU BEYOND,

THE WINDS,

THE STARS,

BEYOND THE GALAXIES,

EVERYTHING THAT I HAVE DONE,

I HAVE TRIED,

TO DO IT,

TO GIVE YOU ALL,

THE LOVE,

FROM MY SPIRIT,

FROM MY HEART,

FROM MY SOUL,

NO!

I AM NOT PERFECT,

BUT I HAVE BEEN WITH YOU,

FROM THE START,

YOU DIDN'T HAVE TO ASK,

WHO IS MY FATHER,

I HAVE STOOD THERE,

SOMETIMES THROUGH,

FLOODING WATERS,

THAT YOU DON'T UNDERSTAND,

I TRIED TO BE,

YOUR INSPIRATION,

I HAVE ENJOYED THE INNOCENCE,

OF YOUR YOUTH,

LAUGHS AND SMILES,

OF YOUR LOVE,

WHAT IS IT,

THAT HAS TAKEN YOU,

AWAY FROM ME,

I CAN NO LONGER,

FEEL YOUR LOVE,

DID I DO WRONG,

WHEN DID I,

JUST BECOME A FATHER,

BUT,

NO LONGER YOUR FRIEND,

I DON'T CONTROL THE WORLD,

MY LIFE,

HAS BEEN OPEN TO YOU,

I GREW UP IN A WORLD,

DIFFERENT THAN YOU,

BUT I THOUGHT,

LOVE WOULD,

ALWAYS BE LOVE,

BEFORE I WAS BORN,

EVEN PAST YOUR BIRTH TOO,

YOU WERE EACH BORN,

WITH DIFFERENT,

CIRCUMSTANCES,

BUT THAT NEVER,

CHANGED MY LOVE,

FOR YOU,

I NEVER WAIVERD,

IN DEFENSE OF YOU,

IN ANY FIGHT,

FOR YOU,

YOUR LIFE,

IS NOT MY LIFE,

I TRIED TO TEACH,

YOU WHAT I KNEW,

I NEVER ASKED FOR MUCH,

JUST WANTED THE BEST,

FOR EACH,

AND,

EVERYONE OF YOU,

I LIVE IN THE PRESENCE,

SILENT OF YOUR,

LAUGHS OR SMILES,

I DON'T GET A,

I LOVE YOU,

WHAT IS IT,

THAT I HAVE DONE,

FOR EACH OF YOU,

TO FEEL,

WITH YOUR DAD,

YOU ARE DONE,

I RESPECT YOUR,

RIGHT TO FEEL,

I HAVE TO RESPECT,

YOUR RIGHT TO JUDGE ME,

BUT WHEN I DON'T

KNOW WHY,

YOU DON'T LOVE ME,

I FEEL THAT,

IN YOUR LIFE,

I HAVE FAILED THEE,

I JUST ASK YOU,

TO FORGIVE ME,

I AM THE FATHER,

WITH NO CHILDREN..........

L. STANLEY BASCOMB OCT. 17,2016 ©

FEEL ME
EVERYDAY FAMILY

I SIT HERE THINKING OF WHAT I COULD SAY,

FOR YOU TO UNDERSTAND,

TO ME CHRISTMAS IS HEIGHTENED,

BY EXPECTATION AND OR MATERIAL,

FOR ONE WHOLE DAY,

THEY SAY THAT CHRISTMAS,

BRINGS THE SPIRIT OF LOVE,

OF GIVING AND CARING,

BUT IF YOU DIDN'T,

HAVE THAT SPIRIT,

DIDN'T HAVE THAT,

CARING OR GIVING,

OR THAT LOVE,

IN YOUR HEART,

THE DAY BEFORE,

AND IT DOESN'T CONTINUE,

THE 363 DAYS AFTER,

WHAT ARE YOU TRULY?

CELEBRATING,

THE SPIRIT OF LOVE,

HAS NO TRADITION,

DOESN'T LEAVE,

AFTER 1 DAY,

NOTHING IS PERFECT,

NOTHING REMAINS THE SAME,

I HAVE NOBODY HERE,

WITH ME,

BUT I FEEL YOU ALL,

I FEEL COMFORTABLE,

I FEEL GOOD,

CAUSE YOU DIDN'T,

HAVE TO WAIT,

FOR THAT 1 DAY CALLED,

CHRISTMAS,

FOR YOUR STOCKING,

TO BE FULFILLED,

WITH THE LOVE,

THAT I HAVE,

FOR EACH AND EVERYONE,

OF YOU..........

L. STANLEY BASCOMB (c) 2010

FOREVER OURS

EARTH DAYS MAY PASS,
BUT OUR SPIRITS AND LOVE,
WILL FOREVER LAST..........

L. STANLEY BASCOMB © 2010

I AM YOU

EVEN THOUGH I BARELY,

GOT TO KNOW YOU,

CAN'T REMEMBER,

YOUR MOTHERLY TOUCH,

YOU HAVE SHARED,

WITH ME,

ONE OF,

YOUR GIFTS,

THE GIFT TO WRITE,

TO EXPRESS,

MY LOVES,

AND YES,

MY FEARS,

YOU HAVE GIVEN ME,

SO VERY MUCH,

I TRY TO HIDE,

MY TEARS,

BUT AS I LOOK,

AT A PICTURE,

OF YOUR FACE,

I CAN'T HELP,

BUT TO SMILE,

I FEEL SO MUCH OF,

YOUR SPIRITUAL,

HAS FOUND MY SOUL,

OBVIOUSLY,

I KNOW MORE NOW,

THAN I KNEW BEFORE,

IT'S NOT ALWAYS,

WHAT YOU CAN,

SEE WITH YOUR EYES,

IT'S HOPE,

LOVE,

AND DETERMINATION,

THAT IS THE BOND,

TO OUR TIES,

I LOVE YOU,

MY MOTHER,

BECAUSE IN THE END,

I CAN SHARE YOU,

WITH THE WORLD,

WITH THE WORDS,

YOU HELP ME,

BLEND..........

DEDICATED TO FLORA

L. STANLEY BASCOMB OCT. 17, 2016 ©

JAVONTAE BASCOMB

OUR JOURNEY BEGAN ON A THURSDAY, JUNE 25, 1998,

SINCE THAT TIME I HAVE WATCHED YOU BECOME AN ACHIEVER,

YOU HAVE BEEN WELL RESPECTED, BALANCED, THOUGHTFUL, RESPECTFUL AND YOU DID IT YOUR WAY, BEING A LEADER OF YOURSELF, NOT A FOLLOWER OF OTHERS.

WORDS WILL NEVER BE ABLE TO EXPRESS MY LOVE FOR YOU MY SON, THE CARE AND RESPECT THAT I HAVE FOR YOU JAVONTAE, I ASK THIS AND HOPE THAT YOU CARRY ME, IN YOUR HEART, I HOPE THAT I HAVE EARNED THAT FROM YOU, THE LOVE THAT I HAVE FOR YOU, WILL TRANSCEND PAST THE BOUNDARIES OF TIME.

THERE IS ONE LAST LESSON THAT I WANT TO LEAVE TO YOU,

BE AWARE OF WHO AND WHAT IS AROUND YOU IN YOUR PERSONAL LIFE.

HAPPY GRADUATION, YOUR REAL JOURNEY STARTS NOW..........

DAD!

L. STANLEY BASCOMB JUNE 14, 2016

LAST NIGHT

LAST NIGHT I WROTE A MILLION POEMS,

BUT I COULDN'T FINISH ONE, LAST NIGHT I LISTENED TO A

THOUSAND SONGS,

I WENT BACK TO MARVIN GAYE,

OHH MERCY MERCY ME,

CURTIS MAYFIELD,

KEEP IT PUSHIN,

ARETHA FRANKLIN,

RESPECT,

EARTH WIND & FIRE,

KEEP YOUR HEAD TO THE SKIES,

I AM NOT HERE TO PREACH TO ANYONE,

I AM NOT HERE TO TEACH ANYONE A LESSON,

I AM NOT HERE TO GIVE WISDOM,

CAUSE MOST OF YOU,

I CAN LEARN FROM,

I JUST WANT TO GO BACK TO,

OLD FASHION,

OLD STYLE,

DOWN HOME LOVE,

I AM NOT THE FATHER,

THE GLORY,

OR THE AMEN,

I AM JUST A MAN,

I USED TO WALK IN A DARK WORLD,

BUT THE LOVE THAT I HAVE FOR YOU,

AND THE LOVE THAT I HAVE GOTTEN FROM YOU,

EVEN SOME CHOICE WORDS,

FROM YOU,

MY FAMILY AND MY FRIENDS,

GAVE ME A BETTER PATH,

TO UNDERSTAND,

THAT I NEEDED TO FIND RESPECT IN MYSELF,

I AM NOT FINISHED WITH TRYING TO BETTER MYSELF,

THERE WILL BE DAYS THAT I WILL FALL SHORT,

EXCUSE ME,

FORGIVE ME NOW,

FOR THEY WILL COME,

BUT SOMEWHERE, SOMEHOW,

THE TRAIL OF LOVE STARTED UP THIS STEEP MOUNTAIN,

I AM ASKING MY FAMILY,

TO GO WITH ME,

LEND A HAND,

THAT JOURNEY WE CAN TAKE TOGETHER,

CAUSE I CAN'T GET THERE ON MY OWN,

I NEED YOUR HELP,

WILL YOU HELP,

I MISS THAT LOVE,

THERE ARE CHALLENGES IN FRONT OF US,

MY MEASURE OF LOVE DOESN'T HAVE TO BE YOURS,

BUT KNOW THAT YOU HAVE SOME WORTH MEASURING,

I CAN'T GUIDE MINDS,

I CAN'T SOLVE ALL THE HURTS,

PAINS OR MISUNDERSTANDINGS,

BUT WHAT I CAN DO,

IS MAKE SURE,

THOSE HURTS OR PAINS DON'T COME FROM ME,

PURPOSELY,

THAT ONES THAT HAVE PASSED ON,

LEFT THEIR LOVE FOR US TO BORROW FROM,

REACH UP AND GRAB SOME,

IF YOU'RE SUPPLY IS RUNNING LOW,

HERE!

YOU CAN BORROW SOME OF MINE,

BUT AT SOME POINT IN TIME,

IF ONLY A LITTLE BIT OF IT,

PLEASE RETURN IT,

SO THAT I CAN PASS SOME ON,

TO THE NEXT FAMILY MEMBER OR FRIEND,

OR JUST KEEP IT,

BECAUSE IT CAME FROM YOU..........

DEDICATED TO FAMILY

June 1, 2013 © L. STANLEY BASCOMB

LOVE

LOVE

I'VE ALWAYS BEEN MY OWN PERSON,

DIDN'T ALWAYS DO RIGHT,

I DID THE BEST I COULD DO,

NEVER KNEW LOVE,

NEVER KNEW MYSELF,

UNTIL THE CREATOR,

BLESSED ME WITH YOU,

I NEVER KNEW EMOTIONS,

COULD RISE HIGH ABOVE THE SEA,

BUT WHEN I FIRST HELD YOU,

I KNEW A CHANGE WAS MEANT TO BE,

I'VE FOUGHT SO MANY BATTLES,

IN MY LIFE,

BUT ONLY THE CREATOR,

KNOWS I'D GIVE MY LIFE FOR YOU,

YOU CAME IN THIS WORLD SO INNOCENT,

EYES AS BRIGHT AS MORNING DEW,

I JUST WANT YOU TO KNOW,

MY DAUGHTER!!!!!

OHHHHH HOW SO MUCH,

YOUR DAD LOVES YOU,

MY LOVE FOR YOU IS PURE AND TRUE,

PLEASE SEARCH IN YOUR HEART,

SO THAT YOU CAN STAY,

BRAND NEW,

I DON'T KNOW IF I CAN,

WIN THIS BATTLE ON EARTH,

BUT WHEREVER I GO,

YOU WILL BE THERE TOO..........

DEDICATED TO MERCEDES BASCOMB

L. STANLEY BASCOMB © 2010

MOTHER EXTRAORDINARE

MOTHER EXTRAORDINAIRE

YOU ARE CALLED MOMMA, MOM, MOTHER,

WHATEVER IT IS, APPRECIATE HER,

CAUSE THERE IS NO OTHER,

FOR AN OFFSPRING TO LOOK,

JUMP SHOUT, SCREAM AND SAY,

ALL TAKE FULL NOTICE,

CAUSE THERE IS NO REPLAY,

WITH GREAT MEMORIES,

AND LOTS OF RESPECT,

SHE GAVE HER BODY,

GAVE ALL HER WILL,

ENDURED PAIN AND ONE HUGE BILL,

SHE HELD YOU AND ROCKED YOU,

HANDS MORE PRECIOUS THAN GEMS,

EVEN CHANGED YOUR DIAPERS,

FULL OF B.M.,

THERE'S MORE TO THIS WOMAN,

THAN JUST RAISING A CHILD,

SHE'S BEAUTIFUL, THOUGHTFUL AND MILD,

BRIGHT AS SUNSHINE, SOFT AS SNOW,

EYES BIG AND BRIGHT LIKE A DOE,

SHE HAS SEEN GOOD AND SOME BAD,

TO EXPERIENCE LIFE AND STILL GLOW,

SOMETIMES AT A DISADVANTAGE,

BUT TO LOOK AT HER,

YOU WOULD NEVER KNOW,

THIS LADY THAT STANDS,

SO PROUD AND TALL,

REMEMBER SHE TOOK CARE OF YOU,

WHEN YOU WERE BEHIND HER WALL,

TAKE A LOOK,

AND THIS IS TRUE,

SHE GAVE YOUR VERY EXISTENCE TO YOU,

OHH, SUCH A WOMAN,

OHH, SUCH A LADY,

OHH, SUCH A MOTHER,

SOMETIMES SHE'S EVEN CALLED,

BABY..........

DEDICATED TO BLACK MOTHERS

L. STANLEY BASCOMB © 1992

MY FAMILY YOU ARE

I AM HERE, YOU ARE THERE, LET'S BECOME ONE,
BECAUSE IT'S YOUR LOVE I WANT TO SHARE,
TO SAY THIS KNOWING YOU ARE HERE,
MAKES IT SO MUCH BETTER,
THAN WAITING FOR OUR END TO BE NEAR,
ALTHOUGH THE SKIES ARE NOT ALWAYS BLUE,

I KNOW IN MY HEART, I LOVE EACH AND EVERYONE OF YOU,

I LIVE IN THIS TIME, I LIVE IN THIS SPACE,

THE CREATOR KNOWS,

I WOULDN'T TRADE THIS FAMILY FOR ANY OTHER PLACE,

I SEARCH IN MY HEART FOR LOVE WE COULD SHARE,

IF WE KEEP OUT THE HATE OF THE WORLD,

WE COULD TRULY MAKE THIS A FAMILY AFFAIR,

LOOK AROUND YOU, WHAT DO YOU SEE,

IF YOU CAN'T GET ONE THERE,

YOU CAN ALWAYS GET A SMILE FROM ME,

WE MIGHT NOT ALWAYS SEE EYE TO EYE,

BUT I PRAY IT'S OUR HEARTS AND NOT OUR EYES THAT BIND OUR TIES,

MORE THAN JUST YOUR BLOOD FLOWING THROUGH MY VEINS,

YOUR VERY LIFE FLOWS THROUGH MY LIFE,

YOUR HURT IS MY HURT, MY DIME IS YOUR DIME,

THIS I GUARANTEE YOU, PAST THE END OF TIME,

WHATEVER HURT I MAY HAVE CAUSED,

OR MISUNDERSTANDINGS UNRESOLVED,

THE THOUGHTS I HAVE FOR YOU,

MAKES THEM A RAINDROP IN THE SEA,

AS THE SUN RISES,

MY LOVE SILHOUETTES FOR YOU ALL TO SEE..........

L. STANLEY BASCOMB © 1992

MY LOVE

SAYING THAT I LOVE YOU IN WORDS,

REALLY DOESN'T GIVE THE EFFECT,

OR EXCITEMENT THAT COMES,

FROM MY HEART,

FOR YOU,

JUST SOMETIMES,

WHEN YOU HEAR A SONG,

LOOK INTO THE SKIES,

OR,

WHEN YOU ARE EATTING,

YOUR FAVORITE FOOD,

WHEN YOU SEE A SMILE,

ON MY FACE,

WHEN MY SMILE,

IS FACING YOU,

OR WHEN YOU LAUGH,

THAT IS MY EXCITEMENT,

THAT IS MY LOVE FOR YOU..........

L. STANLEY BASCOMB © July 5, 2016

ON TO THE NEXT ONE

THIS IS A BIRTHDAY,

THAT NO MATTER WHO YOU ARE IN THIS FAMILY,

WHETHER YOU THINK ABOUT IT OR NOT,

IS PART OF YOUR BIRTHDAY,

BECAUSE IF THIS BIRTHDAY HAD NEVER COME,

NOT ONE OF US,

NOT TWO OF US,

BUT NONE OF US WOULD BE HERE IN EXISTENCE TODAY,

IT IS A BIRTHDAY THAT HELPED DEFINE,

PART OF WHO WE ARE,

THIS BIRTHDAY IS NOT an OLD BIRTHDAY,

IS REBORN EVERYTIME THIS IS A BIRTHDAY,

IN THIS FAMILY,

THE EXISTANCE OF,

THE WOMAN,

LADY,

WIFE,

MOTHER,

GRANDMOTHER,

GREAT GRANDMOTHER,

GREAT, GREAT, GRANDMOTHER,

SHE IS IN YOU,

AROUND YOU,

SHE WILL HAVE ANOTHER BIRTHDAY,

WHEN THE NEXT,

FAMILY CHILD IS BORN..........

L. STANLEY BASCOMB (c) MARCH 13, 2012

OUR BROTHER,
OUR WONDER,

YOUR PICTURES BEEN TAKEN BY LIGHTNING,

THUNDER CLAPS IT'S APPROVAL OF YOU,

YOU'VE BEEN KISSED BY THE WIND,

YOU'RE BEING CRADLED BY THE CLOUDS,

THE BIRDS SING YOUR SONGS AND THE BEES HUMM ALONG,

THE RAIN HAS WASHED YOUR FACE AND THE SUN HAS PAINTED IT,

GAVE FROM YOURSELF TO HELP US REALIZE OUR DREAMS,

YOU ARE OUR PIONEER THAT KEPT THIS FAMILY STRONG,

YOU HELPED FIGHT OUR BATTLES, RIGHT OR WRONG,

YOU HAD SO MUCH LIMITLESS ENERGY IT SEEMS,

YOU TOOK BREAD FROM YOUR MOUTH TO GIVE A CHILD,

YOU PROTECTED US AND MADE ROUGH ROADS MILD,

TO ONES WHO DON'T KNOW YOU, YOU SEEMED REAL TOUGH,

BUT TO US WHO LOVE YOU, WE KNOW YOU WERE MADE FROM SWEET STUFF,

YOU CLIMBED MANY MOUNTAINS TO HIDE YOUR FEARS,

TRAVELED THE VALLEYS TO EASE YOUR PAIN,

INDIRECTLY WE WERE THE ONES TO GAIN,

WE LOVE YOU MY BROTHER BECAUSE YOU ARE THE ONE,

THAT STEPPED OUT OF YOUSELF,

TO MAKE SURE WE GOT OURS DONE,

YOU DIDN'T ASK FOR MUCH, BUT YOU GAVE PLENTY,

I KNOW IF NEEDED, YOU WOULD TRADE YOUR MILLION DOLLARS,

FOR MY PENNY,

YOU!! YOU WERE YOUR OWN MAN,

EVEN IF NO ONE UNDERSTOOD, YOU STUCK TO YOUR PLAN,

YOU HAD STRENGTH THAT MADE US PROUD,

TO BE ABLE TO SCREAM WITH PRIDE VERY LOUD,

TO CHILDREN YOU WERE JUST A BIG MANCHILD,

YOU HELD THEM, YOU LOVED THEM AND MADE THEM SMILE,

YOU LIVED THROUGH THEM,

BECAUSE THIS WORLD COULDN'T SEE,

YOU CARRIED THE FRESHNESS OF LOVE,

LIKE THE PINE FROM A TREE,

YOU PLAYED A DUAL ROLE IN THIS LIFE,

NOW YOU CAN BE FREE, WITH NO MORE STRIFE,

THIS I SAY TO YOU, AND THIS WILL ALWAYS BE,

TOGETHER, ALL OF US

JUST THAT YOU'RE ABOVE WITH THEE,

MY BROTHER, MY WONDER,

HOLD A PLACE FOR ME..........

DEDICATED TO OUR BROTHER ERDMAN

L. STANLEY BASCOMB © 1992

US

I CAN TALK THE TALK,

CAUSE WITH YOU MY SON,

WE WILL WALK THE WALK,

I WALK WITH YOU IN MY ARMS,

AS THE WINDS CRADLE US,

THE CREATOR PROTECT US FROM EARTHLY HARM,

I KEEP MY HEAD HIGH,

TO WALK WITH DIGNITY,

CONFIDENCE AND SELF RESPECT,

DON'T SAY YOU CAN'T,

JUST ALWAYS TRY,

YOU ARE MY FOOTSTEPS BEHIND ME,

MY ECHO FROM WITHIN,

I'M NOT JUST YOUR FATHER,

I'M ALSO YOUR FRIEND,

WE ARE KINGS OF THE EAST,

KINGS OF THE WEST,

THERE'S NO SUCH THING AS PERFECT,

JUST PLEASE DO YOUR BEST,

WHEN YOU OPEN YOUR MOUTH,

I HEAR THE BLOOM OF SPRING,

YOU OPEN YOUR EYES,

I SEE THE SPARKLE OF HOPE,

WHEN YOU LAUGH,

YOU HOLD OUR FUTURE,

WE WALK TOGETHER NOW,

SPIRIT AND SOUL,

TALK WITH ME MY SON,

I WILL SEE YOU THROUGH,

WHEN YOU TAKE THAT LONG WALK,

I WILL BE THERE TOO..........

DEDICATED TO JAVONTAE BASCOMB

L. STANLEY BASCOMB © 2012

WHAT I AM

I AM STANLEY BASCOMB,

I AM GROWING, I AM A MAN,

I DO THE BEST I POSSIBLY CAN,

AS FAR AWAY AS I CAN SEE,

I KNOW IN MYSELF, THAT MY SOUL IS FREE,

IF I CAN I WILL HELP OTHERS,

HOPEFULLY IT'LL MAKE THEM,

GO HELP OTHERS,

FROM OTHERS LESS FORTUNATE I WILL NOT TAKE,

CAUSE I WOULD LIKE TO KNOW,

THAT I AM NOT A FAKE,

SOMETIMES MY THOUGHTS ARE VERY WILD,

BUT DEEP INSIDE I AM VERY MILD,

THERE ARE TIMES I MIGHT SHED A TEAR,

BUT THERE'S NOTHING IN THIS WORLD I FEAR,

SOMETIMES THERE ARE THINGS I NEGLECT,

THE POWER OF LOVE,

I HAVE SO MUCH RESPECT,

I HAVE PARTS OF ME, THAT ARE GONE AWAY,

ALL I CAN DO IS WAIT AND PRAY,

FOR THIS I WANT FOR EVERYONE,

BE THE BEST AND NUMBER ONE,

I TRY SO HARD NOT TO BLUNDER,

KNOWING THAT AT TIMES I WILL,

PLEASE, UNDERSTAND,

AS BEST YOU CAN,

BARE WITH ME AND I WILL BARE WITH YOU,

FOR IN THIS FAMILY,

WE ARE SOME OF THE CREATOR'S GREATEST WONDERS..........

L. STANLEY BASCOMB

WHEN I'M NOT HERE! CAN I!

BE THE WINDS,

THAT GIVES YOU THAT PUSH TO SUCCESS,

THE THUNDER,

THAT JUMP STARTS YOUR HEART,

WHEN YOUR ENERGY IS LOW,

SING THE SONGS OF THE BIRDS,

FUEL THE FIRE OF THE VOLCANO'S,

TO KEEP YOUR DETERMINATION FLOWING,

WHEN I'M NOT HERE! CAN I,

BE THE BLADE OF GRASS,

TO CUSHION YOU'RE EVERY STEP,

BLOSSOMS IN THE BREEZE,

A FIREFLY'S LIGHT,

SMELL THE VISION,

KEEP IT IN SIGHT,

WHEN I'M NOT HERE! CAN I,

BE THE CLOUDS IN THE SKY

TO MAKE EVERY FALL,

NOT TOO FAR,

LAY ON ME,

SO,

YOU CAN KEEP VISION,

WITH THE STARS,

BE THE RAIN,

TO WASH AWAY YOUR SORROWS,

BE THE SUN,

TO PAINT THE SMILE,

BACK ON YOUR FACE,

WHEN I'M NOT HERE! CAN I,

JUST BE REMEMBERED,

AS A MAN THAT TRIED,

EVEN AT TIMES,

OTHERS WONDERED,

WHY I HAD THAT TEAR,

IN MY EYE,

WHEN I'M NOT HERE! CAN I,

BE THE ONE,

THAT CAN STILL,

LOOK IN YOUR EYE,

GIVE YOU A SMILE,

NO MATTER THE DIFFERENCES,

WE MAY HAVE HAD,

KNOW IN MY HEART,

YOUR,

BLOOD IN ME,

DID MAKE A DIFFERENCE,

YOUR VERY EXISTANCE,

WAS MY EXISTANCE,

WHEN I'M NOT HERE! CAN I,

KNOW THAT YOU,

ARE OK!

EVEN IF I HAVE GONE,

AND ON MY WAY,

WHEN I'M NOT HERE! CAN I,

KNOW!

THAT I HAVE BEEN HERE..........

DEDICATED TO MY CHILDREN MERCEDES, MARC, JAVONTAE

L STANLEY BASCOMB © September 18, 2010

WHEN WILL WE LOVE US

CAN I SEE YOU TOMORROW?

I WANTED TO SEE YOU TODAY,

CAN WE TALK,

I'M SURE,

WE CAN FIND SOMETHING TO SAY,

PLEASE DON'T WAIT FOR THE DAY,

WE MIGHT BE,

ON OUR FINAL WAY,

DIDN'T WE LEARN SOMETHING,

IN OUR FAMILY'S

OTHER FATEFUL DAY,

WHEN WILL WE LOVE US,

WILL WE WAIT FOR ME, IN MY SUIT,

SO CUTE,

FOR US TO UNDERSTAND,

THAT WE ARE FROM THE SAME ROOT,

ME IN MY DRESS, THAT WILL NEVER NEED ANOTHER PRESS,

BEFORE I GO TO THAT FINAL ADDRESS,

WHEN WILL WE LOVE US,

WHEN YOU THINK OF US, DON'T BALK,

YOU SMILE WITH AND HUG OTHERS,

DON'T LEAVE ME OUT,

OUR LOVE SHOULD BE MORE SOLID,

THAN ANY ROCK,

WHEN WILL WE LOVE US,

DO YOU REALLY KNOW ME?

WILL WE SEE EACH OTHER AGAIN?

FOR US NOT TO BE SPECIAL,

IS WORST THAN ANY SIN,

WHEN WILL WE LOVE US,

WHY?

CAN'T WE WALK,

SPIRITUALLY, HAND IN HAND,

EVEN IF WE DON'T,

AGREE,

IT'S YOUR LOVE THAT I WANT TO SHARE,

TO TAKE US TO THE PROMISE LAND,

WHEN WILL WE LOVE US,

YOU CLAIM TO HOLD MY LOVE CLOSE,

TRY TO DO YOUR BEST,

IF YOU DON'T TALK TO ME TODAY,

WHAT CAN YOU SAY,

WHEN MY LAST BREATH,

LEAVES MY CHEST,

WHEN WILL WE LOVE US,

IT'S NEVER TO LATE,

I WILL ALWAYS LOVE YOU,

DON'T WAIT TO SAY GOOD WORDS,

AT THAT WOODEN PEW,

DON'T WAIT TO SAY GOOD THINGS,

AFTER WE DIE,

LET US HEAR IT NOW,

CAUSE WE CAN'T HEAR IT THEN,

NO MATTER HOW HARD WE WANT TO TRY,

WHEN WILL WE LOVE US,

THE CREATOR, MOMS AND DADS,

MADE US SIBLINGS,

THIS WE HAD NO CHOICE,

BUT! WOULD IT REALLY HURT,

FOR SOMEONE THAT IS MADE OF YOU,

TO GET A SMILE,

A HUG,

HEAR A FRIENDLY VOICE,

A I LOVE YOU TOO,

IN THAT,

WE TRULY DO HAVE A CHOICE,

WHEN WILL WE TRULY LOVE US..........

L. STANLEY BASCOMB © 2007

YOU DON'T OWE ME

YOU ARE MY CHILD,

MY SPIRIT, MY SOUL,

YOU WERE A BLESSING TO ME,

GAVE ME PURPOSE,

GAVE ME MEANING,

NO MORE SEARCHING,

YOU,

ARE THE GOAL,

I ASKED FOR YOU,

BEFORE YOU KNEW ME,

SEARCHING FOR ANSWERS,

YOU BECAME MY CLUE,

YOU OWE ME NOTHING,

CAUSE I ASKED FOR YOU,

YOU ARE MY CALM,

WHEN I LOOK AT YOU,

I SEE PEACE,

WHEN I HEAR YOU,

I HEAR HOPE,

WHEN I HOLD YOU,

I FEEL LOVE,

YOU OWE ME NOTHING,

YOU ARE MY TREASURE FROM ABOVE,

THE LOVE WE SHARE,

WILL TRAVEL THE STARS,

PAST THE MILKY WAY,

EVEN PAST MARS,

LIFE WAS HERE BEFORE,

BUT YOUR VERY EXISTENCE,

HAS MADE IT MORE,

YOU DON'T OWE ME,

BECAUSE YOU'VE ALREADY GIVEN TO ME……….

DEDICATED TO MERCEDES BASCOMB

L. STANLEY BASCOMB © 1995

YOUR SILENT
WHISPER OF LOVE

From your very start,

The first bud,

That bloomed from our family tree,

We didn't get to see you,

As you became the gleam,

For Mom and Dad to see,

We didn't get to see you,

When you took your first steps,

But i know you hugged us,

As kids we cried and wept,

I don't think we appreciated,

What you have done for us,

In our hours of need,

You have not made any fuss,

You may not have,

Shouted it very loud,

But I hear the Whisper,

You are my Family,

For that I am very proud,

To be the first,

The first of,

Many sisters and brothers,

With love and talent abound,

The love that I have for you,

Needs no earthly sound,

This I hear from you,

And it's not from your mouth,

I don't need to hear you talk,

I will always hear your spirit,

Cause you are from,

The deep deep south,

Right now you are my hero,

I marvel at your strength,

I don't want you to go,

Without knowing,

What you have meant,

You have held your head up high,

You showed no tears,

To this world,

You showed no fears,

At this time,

My human emotions hurt,

But when I feel your spirit,

All I can do is smile,

Without even trying,

Even at this time,

You have taught me so much,

To keep my head up,

No problem is too big,

When I feel the breeze,

I will know it's your touch..........

DEDICATED TO AUDREY (CARTER) BASCOMB

L. STANLEY BASCOMB (c) 2010

THOUGHTFUL POEMS

APPRECIATION

YOU HAVE THE POWER INSIDE OF A HURRICANE,

BUT YOU WHISPER WORDS OF WISDOM,

HOPES, DREAMS,

THAT THE WINDS CARRY NEAR AND FAR,

YOU ARE A UNTOUCHED RESOURCE FROM THE HEAVENS,

A SPRINKLE OF POSITIVE,

THAT TRAVELS A LONG WAY,

YOU HAVE SHOWN MANY YOUNG MEN & WOMEN,

THAT THEY STILL CAN,

BELIEVE IN THEMSELVES,

DARE TO HOPE, DARE TO DREAM,

NO MATTER THE DIFFICULTIES,

THAT LIFE SEEMS TO BRING,

MOST OF ALL,

YOU GIVE A SMILE,

AND SMILES COME BACK TO YOU,

THAT IS THE TREASURES & PLEASURES,

YOU BRING,

YES YOU DO,

YOU ARE HUMBLE, BUT NOT WEAK,

YOU ARE CONFIDENT, BUT NOT COCKY,

YOU CAN SEE PAST THE GLITZ, GLAMOR, BLING,

THE TRAPPINGS OF MATERIAL THINGS,

YOU DON'T NEED AN ENTOURAGE,

GO YOUNG MAN,

ALONG WITH YOUR FRIEND WILL,

YOU DO YOUR OWN THING,

YOU WALK WITH HUMILITY,

KNOWING INSIDE YOURSELF,

YOU CAN MAKE A DIFFERENCE,

NOT ONLY DO YOU HAVE,

PEACE INSIDE YOURSELF,

YOU HAVE BEEN GIVE THE ABILITY,

YOU HAVE GIVEN BACK MORE,

THAN YOU HAVE TAKEN,

YOU HAVE GIVEN US AS A COMMUNITY,

THE HOPE TO MAYBE,

BRING ALONG THE NEXT OBAMA,

GIVE HOPE TO THOSE THAT HAVE GOTTEN PAST,

THE DRAMA,

I SAY THIS WITH PRIDE MY FRIEND,

YOU HAVE BEEN A PLEASURE TO MEET,

TO CONVERSE WITH,

TO HAVE YOU PUT YOUR ARM AROUND MY SHOULDER,

CAUSE I FEEL YOUR SPIRIT,

I AM A OLDER BLACK MAN,

KNOWING THAT THERE IS A SPIRIT,

LIKE YOU,

THAT GIVES HOPE,

TO OUR YOUNG BLACK MEN & WOMEN,

AND OUR VEXT GENERATION,

YOU ARE RESPECTED & APPRECIATED,

MY YOUNG BLACK TALL LEAN BROTHER..........

DEDICATED TO JAMAL CRAWFORD

L. STANLEY BASCOMB AUGUST 10, 2014 ©

BLACKER BEFORE

Even though we were enduring Racism,

Battling Injustice,

Still fighting for Equality,

While Curtis Mayfield,

Was singing?

Keep On Pushing,

We were together,

Calling each other,

Brother and Sister,

Rather than,

Nigga and Bitches,

We had a common bond,

We wore our conks,

And our naturals

Ate our baloney and

Syrup sandwiches,

We had to fight the Klan,

So why now,

Do we have to fear?

Another so called Brother,

We may have made some grounds,

By sacrifice and protest,

But how far have we truly come,

When a white boy,

Is safer,

Than a young black boy,

In our own so called hood,

What have we accomplished?

From our slavery days shackled,

To our civil right marches,

When our ancestors,

Marched from the south,

To the north,

Bitten by dogs,

Bashed by police batons,

Now young blacks,

Can't walk,

A street beyond,

Bring me back to the days,

Of pain from Injustice,

From others than,

Ourselves,

I had the comfort of others,

The bosom of a true black woman,

The strength of the true black man,

That fought the injustices,

Throughout this nation,

Why now does a young black,

Fight and kill another,

Without any hesitation,

Without even knowing that other,

Black's name,

To be killed for,

Money, drugs,

Material things,

And for the sake of your gang,

Without consciousness,

Without thought,

Of the pain and devastation,

That you cause.

You may have ended a generation,

Of one's family,

Have we lost our spirituality?

For the sake of materiality,

Don't tell me!

You're black,

Just because you have the color,

And hue,

Learn your history,

Knowing of the ones,

Who have fought for you?

Can you let that young black by?

Like you let the white boy through,

The hardest part has been fought,

Take a moment to look at him,

His ancestors fought the same battle,

For you..........

L. STANLEY BASCOMB (c) August 20, 2012

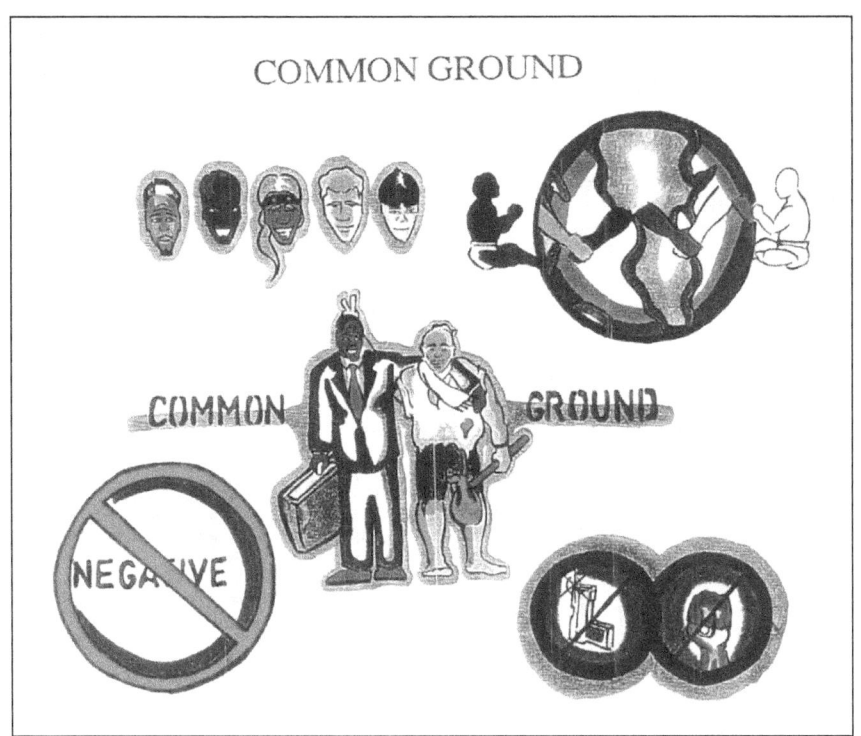

COMMON GROUND

I LOOK IN THIS WORLD,
TO SEE WHAT IT COULD BE,
FROM WHAT I CAN SEE,
THERE'S A LOT OF WASTE,
BUT YET SO MANY POSSIBILITIES,
WE NEED TO WORK TOGETHER,
FOR THIS WORLD TO EXIST,
PLEASE PUT DOWN THE GUNS AND FIST,

WE MUST LOOK PAST COLOR,

PAST OUR ETHNIC BOUNDS,

CAUSE A LAUGH AND SMILE,

LOOKS MUCH NICER THAN FROWNS,

JUST LOOK INSIDE YOURSELF,

I'LL LOOK INSIDE ME,

WE MUST LOOK PAST THE PETTY,

TO FIND WE CAN ALL BE ONE SPIRITUALLY,

EAST COAST, WEST COAST, NORTH OR SOUTH,

WE ALL LIVE IN A COUNTRY,

THAT SHOULD BE ABLE,

TO FEED ANY AND EVERY MOUTH,

WHETHER DIVIDED BY MOUNTAINS VALLEYS,

DESERTS, SEA OR LAND,

IF WE WOULD STAND TOGETHER,

GRASP HOLD OF THE LESS FORTUNATE,

WE CAN REACH AROUND THE WORLD,

AND BACK TO MY HAND,

IT WAS THOUGHT THE WORLD WAS FLAT,

BUT, TODAY WE KNOW IT'S ROUND,

IF WE CAN STOP REACHING FOR THE NEGATIVE,

COMMON GROUND CAN ALWAYS BE FOUND..........

L. STANLEY BASCOMB © 1995

DEDICATION

ALL DREAMS CAN BECOME A REALITY,
AS LONG AS YOU DON'T SLEEP ON THEM..........

L. STANLEY BASCOMB (c) 2007

NUBIAN QUEEN

WHEN I DREAM,

I DREAM FROM THE DARK,

UP ARISES THIS GODDESS,

ONLY WITH HER WILL I EMBARK,

NOT BEHIND ME,

BUT AT MY SIDE,

WHY WALK,

WHEN WE CAN GLIDE,

RESPECT TO YOU IS WHAT I BRING,

BLACK WOMAN,

SO PRECIOUS, SO CONFIDENT,

SO STRONG, SO TRUE,

AN ASPIRATION,

LIKE THE BLOOM OF SPRING,

YOU CREAM, CARAMEL, CHOCOLATE,

WOMAN,

I HAVE LOVED YOU,

SMELLED YOU,

TASTED YOU,

AND THEN,

CAN I BE YOUR MAN,

AND NOT JUST YOUR FRIEND,

BROWN AS THE HONEY,

FLOWINGFROM A TREE,

GOLDEN AS THE RAYS,

THAT GLOW FROM THE SUN,

BLACK AS COAL,

MORE PRECIOUS THAN DIAMONDS,

BRIGHT AS THE LIGHTING,

FLASHING ACROSS THE SKIES,

GIVE ME SOME SWEET POTATO,

FORGET APPLE PIE,

I WILL ENTER YOUR VALLEY,

FOR THE DREAM!!!!!

TO CONTINUE,

I WILL KISS FROM THE NILE,

THE RIVER OF YOUR LOVE,

DON'T LOOK DOWN,

WE'RE FROM ABOVE,

OUR SPIRITS WILL MERGE,

TO BALANCE OUR THOUGHTS,

AND HELP DEFINE,

LOVE AND HAPPINESS,

THROUGH ALL OF TIME,

WE ARE THE UNIVERSE,

WE ARE THE SEA,

PLEASE BLACK WOMAN,

CONTINUE TO STAND WITH ME,

WILL THE DARKNESS REMAIN,

WILL I CONTINUE MY DREAM?

WAKE UP! WAKE UP! BLACK MAN,

LET THE NUBIAN QUEEN,

BECOME A REALITY,

NOT JUST A DREAM..........

L. STANLEY BASCOMB (c) 1988

PRAY FOR OUR CHILDREN

LET'S STOP AND THINK WHAT WE CAN DO,

WE MUST TAKE STEPS TO START NEW,

CHILDREN ARE THE FUTURE,

OF OUR BLACK WORLD,

THEY'RE MORE PRICELESS THAN,

ANY AMOUNT OF MONEY,

GEMS OR PEARLS,

OUR BLACK CHILD IS BORN OF INNOCENCE,

INTO A WORLD OF TURBULENCE
WHETHER IT RAINS OR SHINES,
WE ARE THE ONES, THAT TRAIN THEIR MINDS,
IT MUST BE REMEMBERED BY YOU AND ME,
LIFE IS A GIFT FROM THE CREATOR,
NOT OURS TO OWN,
BUT THE LOVE AND CARE,
THAT WE GIVE THEM,
CAN LAST AN ETERNITY,
TWO CHILDREN PLAYING FOR YEARS,
MATERIAL OR WEALTH NEVER MATTERED,
SOCIETY TAKES OUR CHILDREN,
FROM SPIRITUAL TO MATERIAL,
THE INSTINCT OF LOVE IS SHATTERED,
WHAT WAS NATURAL, IS NOW A LESSON,
YOU'RE NEVER AS GIFTED,
AS WHEN YOU WERE BORN,
FROM LIFTING YOUR HEAD, TO LIFTING A GUN,
THAT INSTINCTIVE CONNECTION IS NOW TORN,
IT'S YOUR RIGHT TO THINK HOW YOU MIGHT,
JUST LOOK AT WHAT WE'VE ACCOMPLISHED,
BOMBS, GUNS AND LASER LIGHTS,
LET THE CHILDREM TEACH ME,
FOR LOVE IS THEIR MIGHT,
LET'S TRY A GAME, THEN YOU TELL ME,
WHEN BORN WE ALL TRADE,

KIDS OF EVERY NATIONALITY,

MY CHILD WILL LOVE YOU,

AS IF THEY WERE HOME WITH ME,

THE GIFT OF LOVE IS BORN,

DOESN'T MATTER IF YOU'RE NATIVE OR FOREIGN,

IT'S HOW WE FILL THAT NEED,

LOVE OR HATE, FAITH OR GREED,

I DO KNOW THIS,

WE MUST LEAVE SOME HOPE,

OR OUR NEXT GENERATION,

WILL CEASE TO EXIST,

WE MUST TAKE STEPS! TO START NEW,

GIVE HOPE TO MANY,

NOT JUST A FEW,

PRAY, PRAY, FOR OUR CHILDREN,

LOVE IS THEIR GIFT,

THAT INSTINCT SO NATURAL,

WILL GIVE THIS WORLD A LIFT..........

L. STANLEY BASCOMB © 1992

DON'T SLEEP ON A DREAM!

All Dreams Can Be Reality!

As Long!

As You Don't Sleep on Them.

L. STANLEY BASCOMB JUNE 25, 1998©

THANK YOU

I THANK YOU FOR THE OPPORTUNITY TO CREATE YOUR VISION,

TO BRING TO FORM, YOUR SPACE ON EARTH,

TO FORM THE FOUNDATION OF YOUR CASTLE,

FOR YOU TO WALK IN HARMONY WITH NATURE,

YOUR LAWN, YOUR TREE'S, YOUR FLOWER'S,

TO SMELL THE BLOSSOMS, THE FRESHNESS OF THE AIR,

WHERE BIRDS WANT TO SING, BEE'S HUMMING ALONG,

WHERE YOUR POSITIVE VISION THRIVES,

I THANK YOU! FOR THE OPPORTUNITY TO MOLD,

YOUR VISION, YOUR DREAM, YOUR INSIGHT,

WHERE THERE IS AN APPRECIATION, COMPLIMENT,

FOR THE WORK THAT YOU HAVE ALLOWED ME TO DO,

I THANK YOU FOR THE OPPORTUNITY TO CREATE YOUR DREAM

AND VISION..........

L. STANLEY BASCOMB (C) 2010

THE WORLD TODAY

THE WORLD TODAY IS A MYSTERIOUS PLAVE,

EVERYONE'S CAUGHT UP IN A BIG RAT RACE,

IT IS A PLACE OF SO MUCH SIN,

ONLY THE CREATOR KNOWS WHAT IT COULD HAVE BEEN,

SCIENTIST SAY LET'S GO UP IN SPACE,

BUT WE WON'T EVEN SAVE OUR OWN HUMAN RACE,

PARENT'S SAY LET'S MAKE OUR CHILDREN FUTURE BRIGHT,

BUT THEY WON'T EVEN TEACH THEM RIGHT,

OUR LEADERS SAY THAT KILLING IS WRONG,

WELL!

HOW DO WE MAKE OUR COUNTRIES STRONG,?

EVERYONE SAYS LET'S MAKE THE WORLD FREE,

BUT WE CONTINUE TO MAKE HUMAN BOUNDARIES,

THE HIP PEOPLE SAY LET'S HAVE A COKE,

THEN WE MAKE SO MUCH POLLUTION,

WE'LL ALL CHOKE,

WE FIRST LEARNED TO SING AND LAUGH,

WHY CAN'T WE MAKE THAT THE GREAT PEACE PATH,

SOME MIGHT SAY ALL THIS MAKES THE WORLD GO ROUND,

BUT I SAY RED, BLACK, WHITE, OR BROWN,

OHH DEAR LORD,

WHERE CAN PEACE, LOVE AND HAPPINESS TRULY BE FOUND......

L. STANLEY BASCOMB © 1988

LOVE POEMS

AM I A FOOL

OHH! SO FRESH AND BRAND NEW,

I KNOW THAT I COULD CHERISH YOU,

AM I A FOOL,

JUST TO EVEN WANT YOU,

WHEN WE HAVEN'T HAD MANY TALKS,

I SIT AND I WONDER,

NOT TOGETHER EVEN FOR ONE WALK,

I HAVE BUILT A BOND WITH YOU,

WITHOUT YOU,

TO BELIEVE THAT RIGHT,

IS ALWAYS RIGHT,

IF YOU DO RIGHT,

THAT WRONG WON'T COME YOUR WAY,

MAYBE YOU WON'T CALL ME TOMORROW,

I DREAMED YOU CALLED ME TODAY,

AM I A FOOL,

TRYING FOR A LADY,

THAT HASN'T HAD,

MANY THOUGHTS ABOUT ME,

WHEN EVERYDAY I THINK OF YOU,

I THINK OF ALL THE GOOD THINGS,

THAT WE COULD DO,

AM I A FOOL,

WHEN I LOOK AT ANOTHER WOMAN,

I THINK ABOUT YOU,

IS IT MY FATE,

ALWAYS TO HOPE,

BUT AT THE END,

I NEVER GET A DATE,

AM I A FOOL,

WHEN I BELIEVE THAT I AM GOOD FOR YOU,

GIVEN A CHANCE,

I WOULD BE,

AM I A FOOL,

I THINK NOT..........

JANUARY 2013 © L. STANLEY BASCOMB

CHANCE LOVE

WHAT WAS IT THAT MADE YOUR EYE'S MEET MINE,

TO STAND THERE IN OUR ETERNITY OF TIME,

WHERE DID THE WORLD GO,

ALL I CAN SEE IS A HEAVENLY GLOW,

I TRY TO SAY HELLO,

YOU'RE SO BEAUTIFUL FROM HEAD TO TOE,

ALL I CAN GET OUT IS A WHISPER,

I FINALLY ASK WHAT IS YOUR NAME,

I SAY TO MYSELF, NO TRICKS, NO GAMES

A SLOW SONG COMES ON,

CAN I HAVE THIS DANCE,

I'M SURE NOW THIS IS MY CHANCE,

TO MAKE YOU MINE,

JUST YOU STANDING HERE CAN INSPIRE ALL OF MANKIND,

I'M FLOATING ON CLOUDS AS YOU TAKE MY HAND,

THE SONG IS DEEP AND SLOW,

MY SOUL IS GONE,

IT'S IN YOUR HANDS,

YOUR TOUCH EMBRACES ALL THAT I AM,

I CAN FEEL A RIVER FLOW THROUGH ME,

THE SOUND OF THUNDER POUNDS IN MY HEART,

LIGHTING FLASHING THROUGH MY MIND,

THERE'S NO SUCH THING AS TIME,

WE WALK OFF HAND IN HAND,

AGAIN IT'S OUR ETERNITY WHERE WE STAND,

CAN I SEE YOU AGAIN,

YOU SAY, I'M JUST HERE TO DANCE,

I'M NOT READY TO TAKE THAT CHANCE,

SHE GLIDES AWAY LIKE A HEAVENLY DOVE,

THE SILENCE BECOMES SILENT,

IT'S JUST CHANCE LOVE..........

L. STANLEY BASCOMB © 1988

DID YOU KNOW?

DID YOU KNOW?   I ADORE YOU,
THROUGH THE HILLS, VALLEYS,
SEAS AND PLAINS,
LET ME EXPLORE YOU,
DID YOU KNOW?   THIS MAN DREAMS OF YOU,
THAT KNOWS IN HIS HEART,
SOME DREAMS COME TRUE,
DID YOU KNOW?   THAT DREAMS CAN BECOME REALITY,
I HAVE MORE CARE FOR YOU,
THAN BRANCHES ON THE LARGEST TREE,
DID YOU KNOW?   WHEN I LOOK IN YOUR EYES,
I SEE THE BLOOM OF SPRING,
THE FLASH OF NEON FOUNTAINS,
A PASSION LIT BE FIREFLIES,
DID YOU KNOW?   WHEN I SEE YOUR SMILE,
IT'S LIKE A BEACON OF LOVE,
A SYMBOL OF PROSPERITY,
A GODDESS FROM THE NILE,
DID YOU KNOW?   WHEN I WALK BY YOUR SIDE,
I SMELL A ROSY BREEZE,
SILK BENEATH YOUR FEET,
FRESH AS THE MORNING TIDE,
DID YOU KNOW?   THE CASCADE FLOW OF YOUR HAIR,
RADIATES LIKE THE STARS,
GLOWS LIKE THE AMBERS OF FIRE,
I CAN'T HELP BUT TO STARE,

DID YOU KNOW?	SOME MIGHT SAY YOU'RE A TEN,
	BUT WHEN I LOOK AT YOU,
	I REMIND THEM,
	TEN IS WHERE YOU FIRST BEGIN,
DID YOU KNOW?	SOMETIMES THE PERSON YOU THINK
	OF THE LEAST,
	THINKS OF YOU THE MOST,
	I CLICK MY GLASS TO YOU,
	YOU ARE MY TOAST,
DID YOU KNOW?	YOU'RE CARAMEL, BEAUTIFUL, DARK
	AND TAN,
	I'M VERY MUCH YOUR FRIEND,
	BUT I WANT TO BE YOUR MAN,
DID YOU KNOW?	WHAT YOU MEAN TO ME,
	WILL LAST THROUGH TIME,
	NOT JUST TOMORROW,
	BUT FOREVER AND ETERNITY……….

L. STANLEY BASCOMB © 1995

DO YOU HAVE A MAN

DO YOU HAVE: A MAN THAT WILL CARESS YOUR FEET,
RUNS YOUR BATH WATER,
COOKS YOU DINNER,
AND NOT EVEN BURN THE MEAT,
DO YOU HAVE: A MAN THAT IS HAPPY, NEAT AND
BOOST YOUR CONFIDENCE,
WANTS ALL YOUR DREAMS,
TODAY, TOMORROW, TO COME TRUE,
DO YOU HAVE: A MAN THAT HAS EASED YOUR FEARS,
LET'S YOU KNOW LOVE CAN BE TRUE,
NOT ONLY DOES HE BELIEVES THE WORD,
HE BELIEVES IN YOU,
DO YOU HAVE: A MAN THAT IS MORE THAN UP TO PAR,
HE HAS GOALS AND DREAMS,
BUT AT NIGHT IN BED,
YOU ARE HIS BRIGHTEST STAR,
DO YOU HAVE: A MAN THAT CAN,
LAUGH WHEN YOU LAUGH,
CRY WHEN YOU CRY,
SAY I DO,
TILL THE DAY I DIE,
DO YOU HAVE: A MAN CARING AND SENSITIVE,
CONFIDENT AND STRONG,
AND BEYOUR MAN,
DOESN'T SAY JUST I CAN,
BUT WE WILL AND WE CAN,

DO YOU HAVE: A MAN PICKING FLOWERS IN THE
MORNING DEW,
SOMEONE WHO DOES'NT FORGET,
PROMISES, ROMANCE, DEDICATION,
THE THINGS THAT MADE A LOVE FOR
TWO..........

L. STANLEY BASCOMB © 2010

DO YOU REALLY HAVE THE TIME

DO YOU REALLY HAVE THE TIME,

TO OPEN YOUR EYES,

ALONG WITH YOUR MIND,

A TREASURE LIKE YOU,

IS VERY HARD TO FIND,

YOU ARE BEAUTIFUL,

BRONZE AND STRONG,

DO YOU REALLY HAVE THE TIME,

YOU SAY ALL THE RIGHT THINGS,

EXPRESS YOURSELF WELL,

THROUGH TEXT,

MAYBE TODAY,

MAYBE TOMORROW,

YOU CAN THROW AWAY YOUR FEARS,

YOU SAY THAT YOU WANT A BETTER MAN,

BUT YOU KEEP STANDING IN THE SAME SHADOWS,

STOP BEING SCARED TO GIVE,

SOME OF YOURSELF,

MOVE FORWARD TO THAT BETTER PLAN,

DO YOU REALLY HAVE THE TIME,

FOR FLOWERS,

A GENUINE SMILE,

A MASSAGE WITH THE CARESS,

A KIND WORD OF ENCOURAGEMENT,

A TINGLE FROM YOUR HEAD,

TO YOUR TOES,

I ASK YOU THIS,

BECAUSE I AM THE MAN,

TO BRING YOU,

WHAT'S REAL,

DON'T LOOK THE OTHER WAY,

BECAUSE YOU MIGHT MISS,

WHAT I,

RESPECT, APPRECAIATE, ADMIRE,

ABOUT YOU,

IT WOULD BE NICE,

IF YOU BRING,

IT BACK TO ME,

BABY GIRL,

WHEN YOU ARE WILLING,

TO GIVE YOUR TIME,

I WILL BE WAITING FOR YOU,

WITH THE DRINK OF LOVIN WITH A TWIST OF LIME,

FOREVER AND THROUGHOUT TIME,

L. STANLEY BASCOMB © JUNE 21, 14

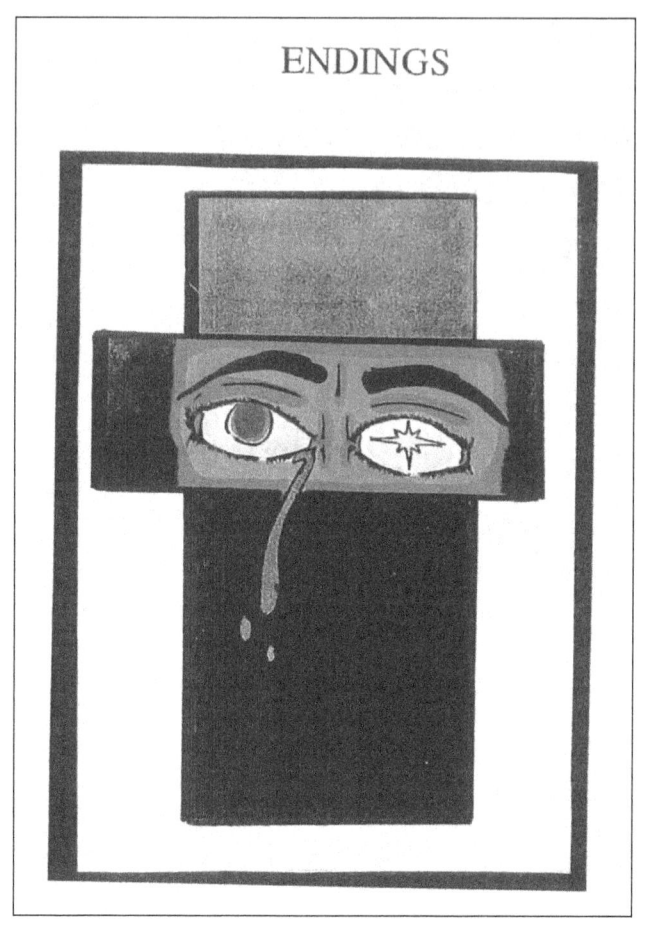

ENDINGS

IT'LL STING TONIGHT,

IT'LL HURT LESS TOMORROW,

DOESN'T MATTER THE HOUR,

PARTING IS SUCH BITTER SORROW,

IF LOVE WAS THERE,

WITH SPIRITS ENTWINED,

BITTER WORDS EXPOUSED,

AT THE END LOVE IS NEVER FAIR,

A HUG BECOMES A SHOVE,

WET TEARS CAN'T DRY,

BEING DOWN MAKES YOU LOOK ABOVE,

AT THE TIME YOU DON'T KNOW WHY,

WE STARTED THIS JOURNEY,

FROM ONE TO TWO,

CAUSE IN THE END,

IT WAS JUST ME AND YOU,

ONE SECOND COUNTS AS AN ETERNITY,

AFTER SO MANY HEAVY SIGHS,

YOU STILL FEEL THE FOOL,

BUT YES,

THAT TWINKLE'S STILL IN YOUR EYES..........

L. STANLEY BASCOMB © 1995

EYES

EYES

IF THERE ARE ANGELS,

THEY WOULD HAVE EYES LIKE YOU,

BRIGHT AS SUNSHINE,

CLEAR AS THE MORNING DEW,

BIG AS THE UNIVERSE,

REFLECTIONS,

SO PURE AND TRUE,

I SO MUCH WANT YOU,

ONCE I WISHED UPON A STAR,

WHEN I LOOKED IN YOUR EYES,

I KNEW THAT STAR,

WAS MORE NEAR THAN FAR,

BLESSED WITH BEAUTY,

FROM HEAD TO TOE,

A BEAUTY THAT COMPLIMENTS,

EVEN YOUR VERY SOUL..........

L. STANLEY BASCOMB © 1995

FREE FLOWIN POEM 4 U

I THOUGHT OF YOU TODAY,

SENT YOU FLOWERS,

YOU MUST HAVE SMELLED THEIR SCENT,

I KISSED THE SKY,

THINKING OF YOU,

I HOPE THIS POEM DOESN'T SOUND STUPID,

BECAUSE IT IS 4 U

I WONDER SOMETIMES,

HOW COULD IT BE,

A WOMAN SO BEAUTIFUL,

A DIAMOND SO RARE,

IS NOT HERE,

WITH ME,

EVEN NOW I CAN SEE YOU,

I'M SORRY,

I CAN'T HELP IT,

I HAVE TO STARE,

NOW I KNOW,

YOU MIGHT NOT BELIEVE IT,

I DIDN'T THINK ABOUT THIS POEM,

I JUST WROTE IT 4 U,

HAVE A GOOD NIGHT SLEEP,

IF YOU FEEL SOMETHING TOUCH YOU,

IT'S JUST ME DREAMING OF YOU..........

L. STANLEY BASCOMB (C) 2010

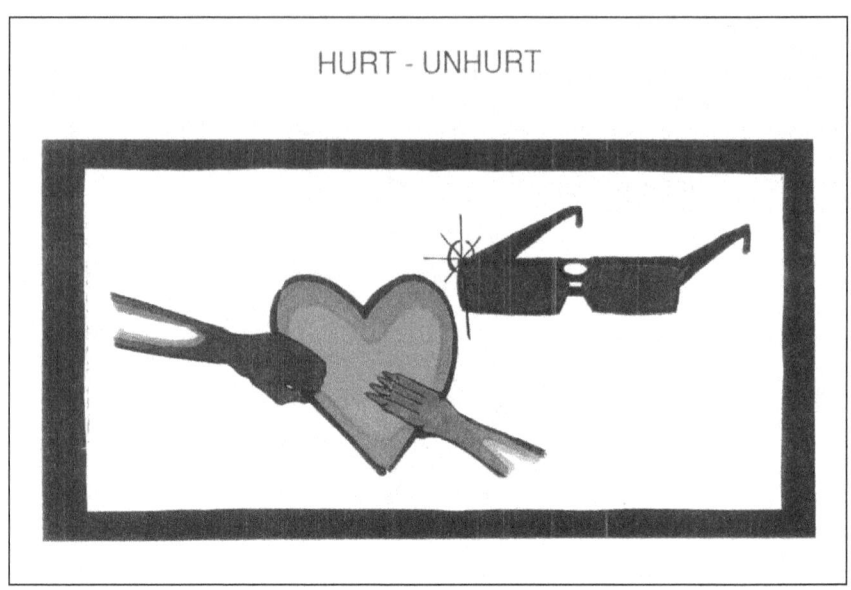

HURT UNHURT

GONE FROM MY EYES,

NOT IN REACH OF MY ARMS,

BUT STILL THE CENTER OF MY HEART,

WHEN YOU LEFT ME,

MY SOUL AND SPIRIT,

WERE TORN APART,

COULD HAVE FELT SORRY,

GAVE UP AND LAYED,

BUT WITH POSITIVE,

THOUGHTS AND INSPIRATIONS,

I AND MY SPIRIT PRAYED,

YOU LEFT ME WITH MORE,

THAN YOU TOOK FROM ME,

A LOVE SO PURE AND TRUE,

BIGGER THAN THE GALAXY,

DEEPER THAN THE BIG DIPPER,

WIDER THAN THE SEA,

MY HEART IS YOURS FOREVER,

YESTERDAY, TODAY, TOMORROW, ETERNITY,

THE WINDS HAVE NO BOUNDARIES,

THEY SWIRL THROUGH TIME,

SOMETHING IN MY HEART,

TELLS ME AGAIN SOMEDAY,

YOU WILL BE MINE..........

L. STANLEY BASCOMB © 1995

HURTS SO GOOD

I SIT ALONE WAITING ON YOUR CALL,

I WANT TO TELL YOU HOW I LOVE YOU,

WANTING TO HOLD YOU CLOSE,

OF ANYONE IN THIS WORLD,

YOU MEAN THE MOST TO ME,

EVERY SONG SINGS YOUR NAME,

EVERY THOUGHT RINGS WITH REMINISING OF YOU,

AND BABY I WANT YOU TO FEEL THE SAME,

IF YOU DON'T THERE IS NO BLAME,

ONE LAST MEMORY,

MAKE IT LAST,

YOU'RE MY FIRST REAL LOVE,

GIVE ME ONE FINAL MEMORY OF YOU,

FOR THAT IS WHAT MY SOUL THRIVES ON,

SPEND THE NIGHT, GREET THE MORNING,

I'LL SHOWER YOU WITH MY LOVE,

EVEN IF THE NEXT DAY RAINS,

SILENT OF TORMENTED PAIN,

SO AT LEAST I'LL KNOW,

BUT YOU KEEP TEASING MY THOUGHTS,

BAITING MY HEART UNTIL YOU'VE TORN ME APART,

PIECE BY PIECE,

EVERY PART OF ME,

SHOUTING LOVE,

THERE IS SO MUCH COMPASSION AND LOVE,

ALL SO NEW, LAY ME DOWN GENTLY,

EVER SO GENTLY, SWEETLY,

LET ME MAKE LOVE TO YOU,

CAUSE YOU ARE MY EVERLASTING LOVE,

YOU'VE BROKEN ME DOWN,

INTO A LITTLE BOY INSIDE,

YEARNING FOR YOUR LOVE AND CARESS..........

L. STANLEY BASCOMB © 1992

I WROTE THIS POEM 4 U

I KNOW THAT I DON'T KNOW YOU,

BUT I AM WRITING THIS POEM 4 U,

YOU MUST UNDERSTAND EVERYTHING I WRITE,

DOESN'T COME OUT OF THE BLUE,

I HAVE BEEN INSPIRED BY YOUR SPIRIT,

YOU'RE SO FRESH AND NEW,

I'VE PLAYED THE GAMES,

WAS CONSIDERED A PLAYER,

BROUGHT ME A TEMPORARY DISTRACTION,

THOUGHT I WAS ON TOP OF IT ALL,

MONEY, WOMEN, CLOTHES, MATERIAL THINGS,

YES!

I DID HAVE PLENTY OF GAME,

BUT AFTER MEETING YOU,

RIGHT NOW MY PLEASURE IS,

JUST BEING TAME,

NOW I WANT YOU TO BE MY ONLY ATTRACTION,

WHAT MORE CAN I SAY,

FROM BEING BORN WITH NOTHING,

TO OPENING MY EYES TO YOU,

LIKE A UNDISCOVERED TREASURE OF TREASURES,

OF THE WORLD AND BEYOND,

IT MIGHT TAKE ME A MINUTE OR TWO,

BUT IN THE END,

YOU WILL KNOW,

I AM WRITING THIS POEM 4 U,

BREATH TAKING,

THE SCENERIES,

THE VIEWS,

NOTHING THAT I HAD TO LEARN,

INSTINCT CAME TO APPRECIATE AND ENJOY,

EVERYTHING A FIRST,

EVERYTHING AT PEACE,

EVERYTHING LIKE, A NEW BEGINNING,

EVEN IF I COULDN'T TOUCH IT,

I COULD VIEW THE BEAUTY OF SATURN'S RINGS,

WHEN I MET YOU,

YOU WERE LIKE THE MORNING DEW,

A BEAUTY, FRESH, SILKY, SMOOTH,

MIXED IN A COLOR HUE,

IT MIGHT TAKE ME A MINUTE, OR TWO,

BUT IN THE END,

YOU WILL KNOW,

I AM WRITING THIS POEM 4 U

YOU TALK WITH THE BREEZE,

LAUGHING WITH THE HUMMING BIRDS,

SMILE AS BRIGHT AS FIREFLIES,

YOUR BEAUTY IS LIKE THE REFLECTIONS,

OF THE RISING AND SETTING OF THE SUN,

I'M SO IN AWE OF YOU,

YOU WERE MY DREAMS AND THOUGHTS,

BEFORE I WAS BORN,

EARTHLY THOUGHTS SAY THAT I AM FOOLISH,

THERE HAS TO BE A CERTAIN,

TIME TO WAIT,

TO APPRECIATE,

YOU CAN'T KNOW RIGHT NOW,

YOU HAVE TO WAIT UNTIL TOMORROW,

AND THE NEXT TOMORROW,

BUT FORGIVE ME,

I CAN'T WAIT,

I HAVE TO KEEP UP WITH THE EARTHS FLOW,

IT MIGHT TAKE ME A MINUTE OR TWO,

BUT IN THE END,

YOU WILL KNOW,

I AM WRITING THIS POEM 4 U,

AND THEN, AND THEN,

IT'S UP TO YOU,

APPRECIATION DOESN'T HAVE TO,

WAIT UNTIIL THE NEXT TOMORROW,

APPRECIATION STARTS WHEN YOU,

TRULY APPRECIATE,

I TRIED TO WAIT,

I KNOW IT TOOK MORE THAN,

A MINUTE OR TWO,

BUT IN THE END,

NOBODY HAS THIS POEM BUT U..........

5/2013 © L. STANLEY BASCOMB

IF I

IF I MADE A MISSTEP IN MY ANXIOUSNESS,

IN WANTING TO KNOW YOU,

I ASK THAT YOU UNDERSTAND,

SOME THINGS TO ME ARE STILL BRAND NEW,

IF I MADE YOU HESITATE,

IN A MOMENT OF TIME,

OF CONFUSION OR MISUNDERSTANDING,

IT WASN'T THAT,

I,

WAS TRYING TO BE IN POWER,

BE INSENSITIVE OR DEMANDING,

SOMETIMES WHEN YOU ARE PLACED,

IN SOMETHING NEW,

IT DOESN'T MEAN IT IS BAD,

OR SHOULDN'T BE FOR YOU,

I CHERISH WHO YOU ARE,

WITHOUT REALLY KNOWING YOU,

KNOWING YOUR SPIRIT,

MY MIND SPINS

MOVES AMONG THE STARS,

IN THE SKIES,

MY PURPOSE IS TO SHOW YOU,

EVEN IF IT WASN'T DONE BEFORE,

THAT YOU ARE VERY SPECIAL,

HAVE YOU HEARD THE WORD,

ADORE,

SOME OF THESE THINGS,

YOU MIGHT NOT UNDERSTAND,

WHAT I AM TRYING TO BRING,

TO YOU,

SOME OF THE OLD SCHOOL,

ALONG WITH THE NEW,

A LADY LIKE YOU,

COMES FAR AND IN BETWEEN,

THAT IS WHY,

I WANT TO SHARE,

GOOD MORNING,

AND,

GOOD NIGHT,

WITH YOU..........

L. STANLEY BASCOMB © JUNE 21, 14

IF YOU EVER WONDERED

SOMETIMES LIFE ISN'T EXACTLY,

LIFE,

SOMETIMES LIFE IS AN AMAZEMENT,

AN ACTUAL,

THAT ISN'T ALWAYS FACTUAL,

HAVE YOU BEEN A DREAM,

WERE YOU ACTUAL LIFE,

FROM THE TIME I MET YOU,

YOU WERE NEVER MINE,

ALTHOUGH THE THOUGHT OF YOU,

FLOATED FOREVER IN MY MIND,

WE AT ONE TIME SHARED OUR,

SON AND DAUGHTER,

BUT NO MATTER HOW I TRIED,

IT NEVER WAS ALLOWED,

THE TIME TO GO FURTHER,

I HAVE LOOKED FOR YEARS,

FOR,

YOUR SPIRIT,

YOUR SMILE,

YOUR FACE,

I SEARCHED ABOVE TO THE STARS,

PAST THIS EARTHLY PLACE,

I TRIED TO CLOSE MY HEART,

TRIED TO OCCCUPY MY MIND,

FOR SOME REASON,

PEACE!

I COULD NEVER FIND,

AT THIS TIME,

EVEN THOUGH I THINK OF YOU,

I MEAN YOU NO DISRESPECT,

DEFINITELY NO HARM,

BUT BEFORE I LEAVE THIS PLACE,

I NEED TO LOOK IN YOUR EYES,

THAT HOLDS ALL OF THAT CHARM,

SOME MAY CALL ME A NUT,

OTHERS MAY CALL ME A FOOL,

BUT SOMETIMES IN THIS LIFE,

IT ISN'T YOUR MIND,

BUT MAYBE YOUR HEART,

THAT MAKES,

THE RULES,

THIS DOESN'T HAVE TO BE,

ROMANCE, LOVE OR EVEN,

I LIKE YOU,

IT'S A SPECIAL PERSON,

THAT I HAD,

ONCE UPON A TIME,

TO SHARE,

SOME LIFE,

SOME THOUGHTS,

SOME LAUGHS,

SOME SMILES,

AND YES!

SOME HURTS,

WITH YOU,

MOST OF ALL,

WE SHARED A BOND,

WE SHARED THE MOST,

IMPORTANT PARTS,

IN OUR LIFE,

OUR CHILDREN,

WHO STILL CALL EACH OTHER,

BROTHER AND SISTER,

BUT!

IT'S MORE SIMPLE THAN THAT,

SIMPLY PUT,

I HAVE MISSED YOU..........

DEDICATED TO LORI CLARK

L. STANLEY BASCOMB © FEBRUARY 16, 2016

IF

IF YOU LOOKED IN MY EYES,

YOU WOULD SEE,

I WOULD WAIT FOR YOU,

NOW, A SECOND FROM NOW,

AND PAST ETERNITY,

THE LOVE I FEEL,

THE TREMBLING OF THOUGHTS,

THAT ONLY YOU CAN STILL,

THE DREAM OF A FUTURE,

THAT TELLS NO LIES,

ALL OF THIS,

IS IN MY EYES,

IF YOU COULD HEAR MY HEART,

YOU COULD FEEL IT,

BEAT YOUR NAME,

KEEP THE RHYTHM OF YOUR PASSION,

WARMING TO YOU LIKE A FLAME,

MY THOUGHTS FOR YOU WILL NEVER PART,

I WISH I HAD YOU,

FROM THE VERY START,

TAKE A LOOK IN MY SOUL,

IT TOOK YOU,

FOR ME,

TO WRITE THIS POEM,

I KNOW I WANT YOU,

MAYBE ONE DAY,

YOU'LL WANT ME,

TODAY YOU MAY SAY MAYBE,

TOMORROW WE CAN GO,

HALF ON A BABY,

I TELL YOU THIS,

CAUSE THIS IS MY GOAL,

FOR YOU AND ME,

TO BE IN THE STARRING ROLE..........

L. STANLEY BASCOMB © 2010

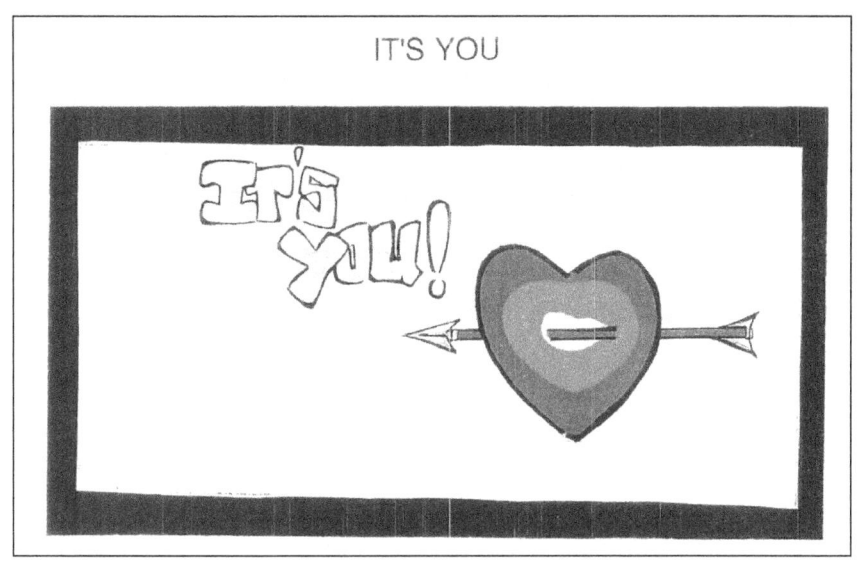

IT'S YOU

YOUR BEAUTY IS LIKE THE MAGIC OF A BEAUTIFUL FLOWER,

YOUR SMILE HOLDS SO MUCH POWER,

YOU ARE A BUNDLE JOY,

MAY YOUR LOVE NOT BE ANYONE'S TOY,

YOU ARE SO FULL OF LOVE,

VERY MUCH LIKE A PEACE DOVE,

TO LOOK AT YOU, TURNS A HEARTBEAT INTO THUNDER,

TO DISRESPECT YOU WOULD BE A SINFUL BLUNDER,

YOUR EYES CAN MAKE THE WILDEST TAME,

NOT TO APPRECIATE YOU WOULD BE A SHAME,

YOUR FEELINGS ARE LIKE A WARM FIRE,

IT'S SO FULL OF WARMTH AND DESIRE,

YOU ARE A LADY THAT SHOULD BE CHERISHED,

CAUSE THE THOUGHT OF YOU COULD NEVER PERISH,

YOU ARE SOMETHING OF AN INSPIRATION,

CAUSE WITH YOU,

THERE COULD ONLY BE A POSITIVE DESTINATION,

IN YOU IS LIKE THE POWER OF LIFE,

THERE'S NO WAY YOU SHOULD HAVE ANY STRIFE,

LIFT YOUR HEAD AND HAVE NO FEAR,

CAUSE GOD HAS MADE YOU VERY DEAR,

THERE IS NO WAY YOU SHOULD HAVE ANY DISTRESS,

CAUSE DEEP INSIDE YOU ARE TRULY A GODDESS,

LIVE YOUR LIFE AND BE THE ONE,

TO SAY YOU ARE THE BEST AND NUMBER ONE..........

L. STANLEY BASCOMB © 1988

LOVIN TIME

HAZE OF THE MORNING CLOUDS MY EYES,

PILLARS OF LAVA SHOOTING THROUGH THE SKIES,

ASCENDING FROM THE EAST AND WEST,

TRIPS OF COLORS, BLUE, YELLOW, ORANGE AND RED,

A FLASH OF LIGHTNING STREAKS ACROSS,

I CAN'T MOVE FROM MY BED,

A SHUTTER OF THUNDER BOOMS,

SILENCE CAN BE HEARD,

WHAT NEXT WILL LOOM,

BIRDS CHIRPING,

BEES BUZZING,

FLOWERS BLOOMING,

IS IT SPRING, CAN SUMMER BE NEAR,

AS STRANGE AS IT SEEMS,

IT'S NOTHING I FEAR,

A FACE OF SERENITY,

DANCES IN THE HAZE,

VISIONS OF A BODY,

I'VE WANTED TO TAME,

WARMTH, WETNESS, TONGUE SO DEEP,

WHAT, WHAT,

IS HER NAME,

I KNOW, I KNOW, I KNOW,

I KISSED HER WITH THE STRONGEST WIND,

CARESSED HER WITH THE SUN,

PENETRATED HER DEEP AS THE SEA,

MADE LOVE IN MY EVERY DREAM,

I HOPE THIS FEELING NEVER ENDS,

TO WAKE UP TO THE SPARKLE IN YOUR EYES,

SMELL THE SWEETNESS OF YOUR LOVE,

TASTE THE VERY ESSENCE OF YOU,

TO HEAR THE FEVER PITCH MOAN OF YOUR SIGHS,

THE HAZE HAS CLEARED,

THE FLASH, THE THUNDER, THE BOOM,

IT'S NOT OUT THERE,

IT'S IN MY HEART AND MIND,

SOME HAVE A DRINK,

WITH A TWIST OF LIME,

THE TASTE FOR ME,

HAS ALWAYS BEEN,

LOVIN TIME..........

L. STANLEY BASCOMB © 1995

MY SOUL IS IN THE CREATOR'S HANDS MY HEART IS IN YOURS

I REMEMBER THE FIRST TIME MY EYES SAW YOU,

THE FIRST TIME MY VOICE,

COMMUNICATED WITH YOUR BEING,

THE FIRST TIME MY ARMS EMBRACED YOU,

THE FIRST TIME MY LIPS TOUCHED YOUR FOREHEAD,

THE FIRST TIME MY HEART WHISPERED YOUR NAME,

THE FIRST TIME MY TEARS RAINED,

THE EMOTIONS OF MY LOVE FOR YOU,

I CAME INTO THIS WORLD,

CREATED AND ONLY TOUCHED BY THE CREATOR,

WITH THE SIMPLEXITY OF,

LAUGHTER, LOVE, JOY, PURITY,

AN INNOCENT CREATION IS WHAT I WAS,

FRESHNESS OF LIFE IS WHAT I BREATHED,

SOUL PURE AS THE MORNING DEW,

THESE ARE GIFTS GIVEN TO ALL BY THE CREATOR,

THEN THE TEACHINGS OF THE WORLD,

PUT ME ON A MERRY-GO ROUND,

SOMETIMES WITH NO MERRY IN IT,

YOU GRASP AHOLD, HOPING NOT TO FALL,

WHAT WAS ONCE SIMPLE AND NATURAL,

BECAME A COMPLEX LEARNING GAME,

WITHOUT A GUIDING LIGHT,

BECAME A DARKNESS OF STUMBLING,

TRIAL AND ERROR,

WELCOME TO MAN'S GIFT TO YOU,

THE LITTLE BOY INSIDE ME,

HAS PROTECTED MY GIFTS,

TOO MANY YEARS MY HEART HAS SAT,

LIKE A HEAVY STONE,

TO KNOW, A LADY, A PERSON LIKE YOU EXISTED,

HAS LET THAT LITTLE BOY,

RENEW A LOVE IN HIS SOUL,

A HEART GONE AWRY,

YOU HAVE BECOME MY KEY,

TO A FRESHNESS IN MY LIFE,

FROM MAN'S COMPLEXITY,

TO THE CREATOR'S SIMPLICITY,

FROM A LEARNED, TO WHAT'S NATURAL,

DON'T BLAME ME, DON'T FAULT ME,

DON'T PUSH ME AWAY,

CAUSE I CAN SEE,

APPRECIATE AND RESPECT YOU,

EVEN BENEATH THE SEA,

FOR YOU ARE A WONDER, A GIFT,

BEYOND EARTH AND ANY BEDROOM DREAMS,

BECAUSE YOU COME FROM A PLACE,

ONLY THE CREATOR HAS SEEN,

AND WHEN HE BRINGS YOU BACK,

I WANT TO BE THERE TO SMILE AT YOU,

I HAVE OPENED MY HEART TO YOU,

BECAUSE THE CREATOR HAS GIVEN ME,

A HEART THAT I CAN SHARE,

I OPEN MY SOUL,

BECAUSE I WANT TO SHARE WITH YOU,

THE ESSENCE OF WHO I AM,

I KNOW YOU DON'T FEEL WHAT I FEEL,

MY LOVE FOR YOU IS NOT SET,

BY THE STANDARD OF EARTH OR MAN,

IT IS MY GIFT FROM MY CREATOR,

THAT I WANT TO SHARE WITH YOU,

BUT MAYBE,

IF YOU HOLD MY HEART AWHILE,

TOUCH THE PURENESS IN MY SOUL,

FOR THE LOVE I HAVE FOR YOU,

MAYBE, JUST MAYBE,

YOU WILL OPEN YOURS,

WELCOME ME IN,

BACK TO THE SIMPLE JOYS,

PURENESS OF THE MORNING DEW,

WILL GIVE US A LOVE TO SHARE,

ONLY SHARED BY A SPECIAL FEW,

IF BY CHANCE I DIE WITHOUT,

BEING ABLE TO SHARE THIS WITH YOU,

THAT'S OK, I'M NOT ASHAMED,

I'LL TAKE IT BACK TO THE CREATOR,

ASK FOR IT TO BE SAVED,

FOR WHEN YOU FIND A LOVE,

YOU WANT FOR YOU,

I ONLY ASK ONE THING OF YOU,

NEVER DOUBT MY LOVE,

NEVER THINK OF ME,

AS A FOOL……….

L. STANLEY BASCOMB © 2010

NEW BEGINNING

I HAVE MET YOU,

BUT I STILL DON'T KNOW YOU,

YOU HAVE RISEN IN MY HEART,

I HAVE HAD DREAMS OF YOU,

BEFORE THIS START,

SOMETIMES,

I HEAR THE HESITATIONS,

IN YOUR VOICE,

LONG BEFORE I MET YOU,

A LADY LIKE YOU,

HAS BEEN MY CHOICE,

NO MATTER,

THE WINDS AND THE SKIES,

BETWEEN US,

THE NUMBERS,

THE LANGUAGE,

BETWEEN US,

I FEAR,

NO IF'S OR WHY'S,

YOU HAVE THE BEAUTY,

OF A SUNRISE,

THE SPIRIT,

SKIES ABOVE,

YOU HAVE EARNED,

THE RIGHT,

TO BE YOU,

TO BE IN YOUR SPACE,

TO BE APPRECIATED,

DON'T TAKE YOUR,

EARTH NUMBERS,

TO HUMBLE YOURSELF,

IN FACT,

IT,

TELLS THE WORLD,

THAT YOUR,

BEAUTY,

IS NEVR ENDING,

I WANT TO BE,

YOUR,

NEW BEGINNING..........

L. STANLEY BASCOMB © OCT. 4, 2016

OUR LOVE

WILL OUR LOVE,
RADIATE WARM LIKE THE SUN ABOVE,
WHISPER LIKE A SOFT BREEZE,
ECHO THROUGHOUT THE WORLD,
RIPPLE WITH THE EVENING TIDE,
WILL OUR LOVE,
SPARKLE AMONG THE STARS ABOVE,
LIGHT OUR REFLECTION OF LOVE BY THE MOON,
UPON THE SEASHORE,
TWINKLE WITH THE DANCE OF THE FIREFLIES,
WILL OUR LOVE,
BE THE VERSE OF A SONG,
THE STRUM OF A HARP,
VOICE OF A SINGER,
A DRUM,
BEATING OUR LOVE FOREVER,
WILL OUR LOVE,
HELP MAKE THE DIFFERENCE BETWEEN,
NIGHT AND DAY,
TAKE OUR WISH AND MAKE IT COME TRUE,
MY LOVE CANNOT FLY,
UNLESS YOU PROVIDE ME,
WITH A SKY,

L. STANLEY BASCOMB © 2007

PLEASE DON'T DISLIKE ME, I AM JUST A MAN

NOBODY GAVE ME THE GUIDELINES TO FEELINGS,

THOUGHT IT WAS SOMETHING NATURAL,

THAT I COULD FEEL,

NOW I HAVE TO ADDRESS MY THOUGHTS, MISINTERPRETED

FEELINGS,

SO BRAND NEW,

I NEVER MEANT THIS TO BE A PROBLEM TO YOU,

I WOULD JUUMP OVER MOUNTAINS, SWAMPS,

HELL'S FIRES,

TO MAKE YOUR MANY PROBLEMS,

JUST A FEW,

I UNDERSTAND THAT I WENT ABOUT THIS WRONG,

IT HAPPENED SO SUDDENLY,

LIKE A FLASH OF LIGHTING ACROSS THE SKY,

PLEASE DON'T DISLIKE ME,

I AM JUST A MAN,

I HAVE NOTHING BUT THE UTMOST RESPECT FOR YOU,

I DON'T KNOW WHO I AM RIGHT NOW,

IF YOU COULD SEE IN MY SOUL AND HEART,

TO UNDERSTAND MY EXPERIENCES IN LIFE,

THAT ME AND THE NEGATIVE,

ARE VERY FAR APART,

I HAVE APOLOGIZED TO YOU,

EVEN THOUGH I DON'T KNOW WHY,

WHAT I WAS SAYING TO YOU LADY,

YOU BELONG UP ABOVE WITH THE,

STARS AND THE SKIES,

BEYOND EARTH'S BOUNDARIES,

FROM DISHONESTY AND LIES,

I THOUGHT I COULD BRING YOU,

THE POSITIVE APPRECIATION OF A BLACK WOMAN,

SOME HAVE BEEN LULLED TO SLEEP,

NOT TO THINK AND HOPE FOR THE BEST,

RATHER THAN BELIEVE,

THE BEST SHOULD BE A GIVEN,

PLEASE DON'T DISLIKE ME,

I AM JUST A MAN,

THAT JUST WANTED YOU TO KNOW AND FEEL,

HIGHER THAN AN MOUNTAIN,

IN MY EYES YOU STAND,

IF I HAVE DONE SOMETHING WRONG,

THAT WRONG WAS FROM TRYING,

TO DO RIGHT,

WHERE EVERY MORNING YOU WAKE,

THE BIRDS SING YOU A BEAUTIFUL SONG,

PLEASE DON'T DISLIKE ME,

I AM JUST A MAN,

THAT HAD DREAMS AND HOPE ABOUT YOU,

I GUESS THAT I JUST DIDN'T HAVE,

THE BEST PLAN..........

L. STANLEY BASCOMB (c) AUGUST 2012

REACHING UP, REACHING OUT

WHAT I COULD BRING TO YOU,

IS A RESPECT,

FROM THE DEPTH OF MY SOUL,

AN ACKNOWLEDGEMENT OF YOUR BEAUTY,

UNDERSTANDING OF WHO YOU ARE,

NO STEPS BACKWARDS,

JUST MOVING FORWARD,

TOWARDS A COMMON GOAL,

I LIKE WHAT I SEE,

I LOVE WHAT I HEAR,

PLEASE GIVE ME THE CHANCE,

TO EASE YOUR FEARS,

A SOFT TOUCH,

A WARM SMILE,

SMELL THE AIR,

HEAR MY WHISPER IN THE WIND,

I WANT TO BE YOUR MAN,

AND FOREVER BE YOUR FRIEND,

I MELT LIKE ICE CREAM,

AT THE VERY THOUGHT OF YOU,

IF YOU COULD READ MY HEART,

YOU WOULD KNOW,

WHAT I FEEL IS SO TRUE..........

L. STANLEY BASCOMB © 2010

REALITY OF LOVE

REALITY OF LOVE

TO BELIEVE THAT SOMEDAY YOU WOULD BE WITH ME,

IS NOT VERY SMART,

BUT I'VE CARED, RESPECTED AND ADMIRED YOU,

FROM THE VERY START,

YOU'VE MADE ME WONDER IF MY MIND IS RIGHT,

BECAUSE I GET SO EXCITED AT YOUR VERY SIGHT,

I'VE NEVER TOUCHED YOU, HELD YOU,

OR KISSED YOUR LIPS,

FOR IN MY DREAMS WE'VE MADE LOVE LIKE A TOTAL ECLIPSE,

I KNOW YOUR HEARTS OUT THERE,

NOT YET WITH ME,

THE LOVE I COULD SHOW IS MADE FROM DESTINY,

YOU FLASH IIN MY MIND, MORE THAN HERE AND THERE,

TO BE WITH YOU WOULD BE THE ULTIMATE AFFAIR,

I WOULDN'T TRADE YOU FOR,

WOMEN, MONEY OR GOLD,

CAUSE WHEN THE CREATOR MADE YOU,

HE BROKE THE MOLD,

I KNOW YOU COULD LOVE ME,

CAUSE THIS I BRING,

A LOVE SO TRUE,

ONLY THE BIRDS AND THE BEES COULD SING,

THERE IS A PART OF ME THAT SAYS NO WAY,

YESTERDAY IS GONE,

TOMORROWS NOT HERE,

I'LL ALWAYS THINK OF YOU TODAY,

I MAY JUST FOREVER BE YOUR WANT TO BE,

IN MY SOUL WHAT I FEEL FOR YOU FLOWS FREE,

IF WE NEVER SEE EACH OTHER AND NEVER TOUCH,

NOW YOU KNOW THAT,

THERE IS SOMEONE WHO COULD LOVE YOU SO VERY MUCH,

AND MAYBE TO YOU THIS ISN'T REAL,

IT'LL BE THERE WHEN THE WINDS STAND STILL,

I WRITE THIS TO YOU,

CAUSE I NEVER WANT TO WONDER,

IF I DIDN'T TAKE THIS CHANCE,

AND NOT TO REALIZE,

OR RECOGNIZE,

YOU ARE ONE OF GOD'S GREATEST WONDERS..........

L. STANLEY BASCOMB © 1992

SPECIAL

SPECIAL IS A THOUGHT THAT WILL NEVER PERISH,

IT'S BECAUSE OF YOU,

THAT I WILL ALWAYS CHERISH,

YOU ARE IN MY DREAMS,

I AM A KING AND YOU ARE MY QUEEN,

YOU HAVE MADE ME OBLIVIOUS TO ALL OTHER THINGS,

YOUR SMILE OHH,

IT MAKES ME FEEL SO MEEK AND MILD,

VERY MUCH LIKE A SMALL CHILD,

SPECIAL ISN'T SOMETHING YOU CAN ALWAYS HEAR,

BUT WHEN I HOLD YOU BABY,

YOU CAN ALWAYS FEEL IT NEAR,

SPECIAL WITH YOU IS NOT JUST A NOTION,

IT MAKES US,

POETRY IN MOTION,

IT'S NOT SOMETHING YOU CAN ALWAYS SEE,

BUT BABY, BABY, BABY,

OUR LOVE IS BIGGER THAN ANY SEA,

SPECIAL WILL ALWAYS BE YOU AND ME..........

L. STANLEY BASCOMB © 1988

THE BEAUTY OF U

You amaze the sun,

You are one of the stars,

That amass the skies,

You have danced with the rhythm,

Of our ancestors,

Made the drums,

Change to a slow beat,

Made the passions,

From the dance

Hot from your heat,

You are the scent,

From fresh blossoms,

To a newly ripe peach,

Within!

You are soft as a still breeze,

A smile that radiates,

Like a flash of lighting,

Moving along,

With the birds and the bee's

The beauty on the inside,

Only enhances the beauty,

On the outside,

That I want to touch,

That I need to embrace,

Swim in the fountain,

Of your love,

There isn't a down,

It's all above,

You are a treasure,

That doesn't come often,

If at all,

I made this poem,

For you,

No matter how many words,

I use,

I can't say it all,

Just want you to know,

There is an appreciation,

Of you,

That can't be repeated,

Or duplicated at all..........

L. STANLEY BASCOMB © 10/15/15

TOUCH

YOU LOOK AT ME AS ONE OF,

ONE HUNDRED AND TWO,

I LOOK AT YOU AS JUST ONE AND ONLY YOU,

OTHERS MAY GET YOUR TIME,

AND BE ABLE TO TOUCH,

I JUST WANT YOU TO HAVE SO VERY MUCH,

MOST SEE YOU FROM THE OUTSIDE IN,

I LOOK T O THE INSIDE WHERE THE GOOD LORDS WORK

BEGINS,

I MAY NOT GET NEAR AND PROBABLY NOT CLOSE,

BUT TO YOU I WILL RAISE MY GLASS AND SAY A TOAST,

THIS I SAY WITH FAITH AND NO FEAR,

YOU ARE SPECIAL TO ME AND VERY DEAR,

YOU MUST SEE SOMETHING THAT YOU THINK I LACK,

I'LL STILL BE THERE WHEN YOU START LOOKING BACK,

WHEN THAT RUMBLE INSIDE YOU STARTS TO SLOW,

HEAVEN WILL TAKE OVER AND YOU WILL GLOW,

WHEN THE WINDS AND THE SEAS STAND STILL,

YOU WILL REALIZE,

THIS FEELING I HAVE FOR YOU,

WILL STILL BE REAL..........

L. STANLEY BASCOMB © 1992

WHY?

WHY? DO I WANT YOU?

WHY? DO I SIGH?

WHY? DO I FEEL?

LIKE A LITTLE BOY INSIDE,

WHEN I LOOK IN YOUR EYES?

WHY? DO I WISH YOU WERE HERE,

FOR ALL TO SEE,

I'M SO DEEP IN THOUGHT OF YOU,

WHY? OHH MERCY, MERCY, ME,

WHY? DO I THINK OF YOU?

WHEN YOU'RE NEVER HERE,

PLEASE GIVE ME YOUR HAND,

I WILL GUIDE YOU,

FROM YOUR FEARS,

FROM YOUR HURTS,

FROM YOUR TEARS,

WHY? DID I MEET YOU?

WHY? DID I SEE YOU AGAIN?

IT'S HARD NOT BEING YOUR MAN,

BUT, I'M TRYING TO BE YOUR FRIEND,

WHY? DON'T YOU LOOK AT ME,

WHY? CAN'T YOU SEE,

I'M NOT HERE TO HURT YOU,

I JUST WANT TO BE,

A SMALL BRANCH,

ON YOUR TREE,

WHY? DO I FEEL,

SO NEAR TO YOU,

BUT YET,

YOU'RE SO VERY FAR,

WHY? IN THE SKIES,

HAVE YOU REPLACED,

EVERY STAR..........

L. STANLEY BASCOMB © 2010

The More You Can Do for Yourself

The Less It Gives Anyone the Opportunity

To Do Wrong to You…………

ACKNOWLEDGEMENTS

To my Immediate family, my bloods, my hearts, my loves and even sometimes my hurts.

I hope that somewhere in my life, I have been able to show you love, comfort, understanding, a laugh, a smile, at the end you have a true understanding of who Stanley was, trying to do the positive, but understanding that, maybe at some time, I hurt you in spirit, please read my poem "My Family You Are" that is the best way that I can explain it.

Maya Johnson my special, loving, thoughtful, caring cousin, you have been a blessing for me and Javontae, when no one would open their doors, you did, this world would be a better place if your spirit could spread to others, your spirit has been here before in your Aunt Gloria and I have no doubt she is proud of you as her spirit still flows.

Amy Vance, you were the only other person that opened your doors early for my son Javontae, I appreciate you treating him like your family, I appreciate your 3 daughters treating him like a brother, made sure he got to school and got breakfast, you acted like family, when some blood family didn't give the time.

To my Friend! My Brother!

George E. Noble You were there when I was searching for me, trying to find a way to feed and care for my daughter, you believed in me, trusted me, you gave me hope.

I truly feel as I am a part of your family as, I say this to you and you know me better than many, I know that you truly thought about my soul and tried getting me to church, well believe me, I am at peace with my soul, I regret nothing, but I had to do it the way that was given to me through my life experiences, I hope you never felt disrespected by me.

I lived life doing it the best way that I knew how to, I told you before that I respect and appreciate you, if there is a heaven and I get there, I'm lucky, but that reward isn't what I am seeking for what I did in earthly life, I just did what I felt was respectful, and in my nature to do and knowing what my faults and weaknesses are, caring genuine in my spirit to do, my reward has been seeing so many smiles I have I have had the fortune to give and so many more I have received, even those of people I didn't know.

Love to you and your (my) Family..........

To my friend Joey Thomas, bailed me out of a difficult situation of not having a defensive coach and helped provide the discipline and respect that was needed to help move forward these young black men that we mentored with dreams, hope and aspirations in life, became one of my most special friends in my life..........

To my single best Friend in the world Aaron Lee Sims

Although you are not here physically, you will always be with me in heart and spirit..........

To my Harper & Vaden family, please get a copy of my book, Love you All..........

I have about 100 Nieces, but this is about 2
My beautiful, thoughtful, caring,
Robin & Mai Ling,
One like a Thunder clap, the other like a cool Breeze,
When I hear you say Uncle to me,
It always sounds new and invigorating,
It makes Love shine from the both of you,
No matter the puzzles in your life,
You have always remained Two,I have nothing,
But admiration, appreciation and Love for the both of you,
I am so, so, glad I took that steps to find you,
You have brought a new Special to this Family,
I am Proud to have you in my book The Parameters of Positivity

Uncle Stanley

STOP JUDGEMENT & SCARE TACTICS!

We weren't born into this world as a Group,

We are not leaving this World as a Group,

We all have our own experiences of good and bad, triumphs and mistakes,

We all have our own individual paths in life,

There isn't any such thing as perfection,

You can only try your best to get through this world,

Give respect and appreciate what an individual has gone through,

Because it is impossible to live someone's else life or path,

Mentally physically, emotionally, spiritually,

Because another individual didn't live your path,

Doesn't mean that you can't both arrive at the same Destination,

Hopefully a positive one for you both,

Quit talking like your path is the only one that can be taken, for success,

Success can only be demonstrated by each individual,

We are not machines, manufactured to operate the same way,

We are just individuals, experiences, mind, souls and spirits,

You are only as human as the person, that you are trying to judge,

Most of the time is you wanting to think that you are the better person,

You can lift- up peopled, you can give caring advice to people,

Stop trying to own people,

Perfection doesn't mean You!

We all have the right to be Proud and Thankful of ourselves,

Every individual spirit, only truly knows their journeys, paths, hurts, loves,

No one can Validate your life but You!

You can't make your journey, exist for someone else journey,

When you are deciding, how to control someone else life,

How some of you take pleasure in trying to make someone feel less about themselves,

Because only you have all the answers to judge others,

Obviously, you haven't had the time to look inside your own life,

Maybe that is where you should Start!

L. Stanley Bascomb (6/29/24)

www.ingramcontent.com/pod-product-compliance
Lightning Source LLC
Chambersburg PA
CBHW061754120626
46550CB00005B/1993